NO ADDED SUGAR

On Life, The Apprentice, and
How I Built a Global Fitness
Business from a
School-Hall Dance Class

by

Katie Bulmer-Cooke

Designed & Published by www.ricksmithbooks.com

About Katie Bulmer-Cooke

'The Apprentice' star, entrepreneur and Mum, Katie Bulmer Cooke first made her mark in the business world at the tender age of 16. From creating her own exercise classes she went on to sell her fitness DVD's and programs across 5 continents, becoming a multi award-winning businesswoman in just a decade.

BBC TV's Apprentice 2014 boosted Katie's profile and brought her to national attention as the level-headed Northern lass and queen of the one-liners. Not yet thirty, Katie has nevertheless built an online fitness business that reaches across the world from her hometown of Sunderland, on England's North-East Coast.

Katie's story is one of driven determination to succeed, and an appetite to take on the world and all it has to offer. Her intention is to inspire the new generation of entrepreneurs to believe that *anything and everything* is possible.

Contents

1 - The Littlest Apprentice

If I had to pinpoint the moment when I first realised that my destiny was to be an entrepreneur, it would be the summer of 1990. Madonna was Vogueing, Sinead O'Connor was Comparing, and in my corner of the world, the North East of England, the unlikely combination of Lindisfarne and Paul Gascoigne sang, "Fog on the Tyne is all mine, all mine!" On the football front, England had by modern day standards excelled themselves, by coming fourth in the Italy World Cup, and my local team Sunderland had managed to scrape promotion from the second to the first division via the play-offs.

None of which really mattered much to me, sitting on the dusty wooden floor in St Johns church hall, surrounded by forty-two women of assorted shapes and sizes, clad in garish shades of Lycra, all there for their weekly ritual aerobics class led by me Mam. Leotards, hair scrunchies, pushed down socks; think Olivia Newton-John in *Physical*, except that this was Sunderland, not South Beach, and you'll get the picture. I was four.

Mam always looked The Business. She had the best gear and the best dance shoes. Perfectly coordinated, her thong-backed leotard matched her hair scrunchie. She was my absolute role model. Dad was working away in Aberdeen, so Mam used to take me along to her classes. I'd sit on that dusty floor playing with my Barbie, but I knew, even at that tender age, exactly what I wanted to do for the rest of my life.

I kind of looked the part, too. Fair enough; my leotard hung off me, several sizes too big. I had a toweling headband that was forever slipping down, so that instead of being around my forehead it always ended up dangling around my tiny neck, but I was desperate to follow in Mam's footsteps.

The venue wasn't the most glamorous; a typical church hall with dusty wooden floors and windows that could have benefited from a good clean. The smell of that dingy hall has stayed with me forever. It wasn't particularly nice, but it wasn't particularly nasty either. It was part of the place, and I'm guessing that it smells exactly the same today as it did twenty-five years ago. The smell of nostalgia, and the happiest of memories.

But Mam somehow managed to light up the room and bring that tired old place to life. She'd pack forty gym mats, what seemed to me at the time to be a massive stereo cassette system, and me, an aerobics-mad four year old, into her bright red Ford Fiesta, and off we'd go every Tuesday and Thursday night. She'd spend hours at home mixing up the tapes, starting with the slower warm-up tracks which built steadily through the hour, to the faster stuff which was designed to motivate her followers, because that's what they became, to puff and perspire their way to the end. Everything about it was just fantastic, especially to a wide-eyed four-year old!

Looking back, I think my first serious lesson in business, gleaned exclusively from Mam's example, was Customer Service. Not only was she a fantastic saleswomen, and not at all pushy, but she had a legendary ability to retain customers. Twenty five years later, and well into her fifties, she's still teaching exercise classes in the same town, to many of the same people, though the colourful leotards and pastel leg-warmers have long since given way to more sporting outfits.

Mam knew her customers inside out, and she knew what they needed, even when they didn't know it themselves. Whether they'd come for fitness, to lose weight, or simply for the social aspect, she's always known exactly what to do to give them a great result and keep them coming back for more. She was, and still is, a persuasive and consummate professional.

Down the years she'd always managed to captivate her ladies with the right music choices, the right exercises, and even what she wore, which made her a credible role model both for them, and more especially for me. She instinctively knows how to identify their needs and give them great value. So they've kept coming back every week, religiously, some of them for over a quarter of a century.

As I got a little older, I graduated from a spectator to become her business sidekick. I was given new responsibilities; handing out leaflets about the next classes, collecting the money at the door, until eventually I was old enough to join in with the classes themselves. I would go along and help her carry the mats in, set up the stereo, and every Tuesday and Thursday night I was her Apprentice.

As childhood innocence gave way to my teenage years, I was building a clearer picture of how things worked. When I was little, I remember just being in awe of how Mam could create such an incredible atmosphere, with everyone moving to the music, smiling through the pain. She took an old, rundown, underused space, and turned it into a glittering, glamorous place; somewhere everyone wanted to be, and nobody wanted to leave.

As I grew more aware, I began to understand how much money she was making. She paid ten pounds to hire the hall, and charged everyone two pounds fifty pence to attend the class. Once I had the maths skills, I started to figure out the margins, a valuable lesson that has remained central to my own business ventures. Plus, I started to notice and appreciate all the important little things that she did to keep the ball rolling. She was relentlessly marketing, delivering, and repeating. She had a winning formula, and although it has evolved over the years, the core business disciplines have remained exactly the same.

Back then there was no social media; unless you phoned or called around, the quickest way to communicate with an audience was by sending a letter, which took at least two days to arrive. So it simply wasn't a viable way to run a social business like hers. She was designing and printing leaflets, and then delivering them door to door around the local area. She wasn't using data capture; no Wordpress websites or Facebook Pages. The things we now take for granted simply didn't exist back then.

She was collecting her customers' information whenever she met them. If someone stopped attending class, she'd phone to ask them how they were, mention that she hadn't seen them for a while, and find out why. It was personal service in every sense of the words, a skill that many people and businesses have lost in the ensuing twenty-five years, certainly in mainstream marketing.

These days, people are wholly reliant on e-mail and electronic messaging. They blast out tweets or posts and rely on people seeing them, rather than picking up the phone and finding out why someone hasn't been in for a while, and closing them for a commitment to come back next week.

Nowadays, the world communicates differently, but as I grew my own businesses, I never forgot the important lessons I learned in that dingy church hall. I'll gladly pick up the phone and call someone I haven't seen lately, just to ask how they are and find out if and when they're coming back. Make it personal. It worked for Mam back then, and it still works perfectly for me. These days we call it *retention tools*, part of the huge

Customer Service armory we have at our disposal. Back then there simply wasn't any other way, if you wanted to build something that worked.

At sixteen, I was old enough to take the grandly titled *'Level Two Exercise to Music'* qualification. Mam had heard about an initiative to encourage under-18's to take the course at a significant discount. I recall that it was a not-insignificant £250 for something that would be upwards of a thousand these days. There was absolutely no doubt that I was headed that way, so Mam said she'd pay for the course, and obviously I bit her hand off. She bought it for my 16th birthday, and she still says to this day that it's the best money she's ever spent, because it was the springboard to everything I've been able to do since.

The course was held at Farringdon Primary School hall, in a class that was very similar to how Mam was running hers. No spanky Virgin Active studio for me! More dust, and none too clean windows; dull and dreary when there wasn't anything happening, but exciting and electric when the pulsating music came on and we all started moving.

At sixteen years old I was by far the youngest person on the course. Almost everyone else was over thirty, many of them taking a shot at starting a second career, something they could feel passionate about and which would enable them to escape the drudgery of an office or factory job. My course was held every Saturday, and I remember being unable to sleep on

Friday nights; I was so excited and pumped up about the next day. Boy, was I nervous. But I knew I'd found my niche.

I was constantly practicing the routines at home during the week before going off to my Saturday class. The instructor would set us homework each week, and I was fanatical about making sure that I had absolutely everything buttoned down before I got there. Even though I was the baby of the group, I already had a good grounding from the years of growing up in Mam's classes in the old church hall.

It was only the second or third week of the course and, out of the blue, the instructor informed me that I was going to teach my warm-up to the rest of the class. No pressure then! I practiced all week, but I was too nervous to try it out in front of Mam for rehearsal. To this day I still get embarrassed if she comes to one of my classes, even though my career in the fitness industry has seen such great achievement. I am still star-struck by her.

It wasn't really Dad's cup of tea either, so I used to practice the routines to my friend's dog, or even to the stereo. I'd make up my cassette tape, put it into the player, then I'd stare at the stereo and teach an inanimate object my warm-up, which seemed like the most natural thing in the world back then.

It was always really important to me that I didn't just learn and practice the moves, but also the essential motivational commentary that went along with them. It was my job to *drive* the classes, so I knew I had to practice the words and get everything working in time with the music. You can't shut up for a moment, or the class simply falls apart.

The exercise music of the time was stuff like the Venga Boys, Cher, and Steps; tunes that would make most people cringe these days. But for me, in the moment, it was liberating, inspiring, and uplifting. And it's all there was!

Workout fashion had changed, too, since Mam's early classes in the church hall. Leotards and leg warmers were (sadly) on the way out. Nike had introduced their Nike Women fitness range, with workout pants with flared bottoms, vest tops, and a dazzling array of different trainers. Turquoise and pink begat black, white, and orange, and for the first time women's fitness fashion was making something of a name for itself. Exercise clothing could now be worn on the street without anyone laughing! From the amount of money and marketing that companies like Nike, Reebok, and Adidas were pouring into the industry, the explosive growth of huge gymnasiums, and the fitness fever that was sweeping the country, it was clear that this business was set to boom in the new century. And there was I, little Katie from Sunderland, slap bang in the middle of it all, planning my business future.

2 – Ambition and Realisation

"I freaked out and realised that my business model absolutely sucked"

Mam and Dad always had a really strong work ethic, and I always wanted to work, too. I guess I was a product of my environment. As soon as I was fifteen, we were told at school that we were going to be doing a week of work experience, and I couldn't wait.

I knew already that because I wanted to work in the fitness industry, there was only one place to go, and that was the Sunderland Health and Racquet Club, which was a fantastic modern facility that had only recently opened. By now, Mam held classes there, and it was *brand spanking*, the first time that Sunderland had ever seen a place like this. It had everything; a pool, two studios, a café bar, a restaurant, a function room – everything! Plus, it was the best gym in the North East by far, and I *only* wanted to go there.

I knew that it would be a couple more years before I could do what people do, and move to somewhere with more to offer me. But inside I think I'd already figured out that I had everything I'd need on my doorstep, so there was no burning desire to relocate. In hindsight I'm really glad it worked out that way. I didn't need to move away to find out what I was missing; I got it.

The Club was run by a company called Invicta at

the time, so I got in touch and asked if I could come for work experience. They said yes; I could definitely come, but that they wouldn't be able to place me where I wanted to be, which was in the gym or the studio. At my age, and with no fitness qualifications, I wasn't even on their radar at that stage, and although it was a little disappointing, in hindsight I really had been over-optimistic. Little did I know how hard I'd have to work to get my foot on the ladder, but I guess that's the essence of an apprenticeship, in any trade.

Instead, I was given the impressive title of "Café Bar Food Runner", which basically involved wiping down the forty-odd tables, clearing and laying cutlery, and delivering food. I'd never had a proper title before, so they could have called me anything they wanted; I was on my way into the world of work!

The first thing I learned was that just because a café is inside a health club, it doesn't necessarily follow that it's a healthy place to eat! The biggest sellers weren't salads or chicken, or anything remotely healthy. The meal I served most was Cheesy Chips. You could get them in fat chips, thin chips, or curly fries form. There might be some vague nutritional value if you're training to swim the channel, but as a post-workout carb-load, they leave a lot to be desired!

But despite the contrary menu, I loved the job, even though it was hard. Most of the time I was the only runner in the Café, so the work was punishing, but I threw myself into it. As I was just a schoolgirl on work experience, I was assisting everyone else and I was their little apprentice; eager to learn and - for a fifteen-year old - ruthlessly efficient. I soon worked out the quickest, cleanest way to do everything, and I must have made an impression because at the end of my 'work experience', they said, "Come back when you're sixteen and we'll give you a job."

On my 16th birthday, I went up and signed a contract. Mam went out and bought me some black trousers and flat black shoes, as well as my first work uniform, and then the Club issued me a bright yellow work-shirt and a little black pinny. I was over the moon. I was being paid three pounds eighty-five an hour and I thought I was the richest sixteen year-old in Sunderland. They gave me sixteen hours a week, and I carried on working, alongside going to college. It was great.

But as much as I loved it, I always saw it as a means to getting my foot in the door in the gym and the studio. So, after I'd been there a little while, I started asking the same question; was there a spot opening up on the fitness side? But still the answer remained a flat "No," for all the same reasons; "You're still too young, you haven't got the right experience, and you have no qualifications."

Undeterred, I plugged on in the Café Bar. I'd been there for a few months, and one day Mam told me, "Katie, I've heard that they're going to be running the Exercise to Music course at your work." That was my 16th birthday present.

Little Katie; Right Place, Right Time! This was the game-changer.

****

After 16 weeks of study, I had the certificate. I went straight to see Dionne who was the studio manager.

"Look Dionne, I've got it! I'm seventeen now. *Please* give us a chance. Give us a class?"

Another flat No! She said I was still too young, and even with my certification, without experience it just wasn't enough. I was devastated. All through my training course I'd convinced myself that the certificate was all I'd need to get me started. I crawled away to lick my wounds.

Putting it aside, I carried on working hard in the café, but the desire was burning: I had no Plan B. I passionately wanted fitness as my career. In the end it became clear that I needed to make something happen for myself, so I took a leaf out of Mam's book and set up my first class all on my own.

I was now seventeen, which as every girl knows is about a decade older than fifteen, which was when I started this process. I was driving a blue Nissan "Mighty" Micra (I knew it was mighty because it said so on the sticker in the back window), and I set up my first class just like Mam had done, in Ryhope Boxing

Gym. Like the old church hall, it was not the most glamorous place in the area, which was why it was cheap, and as you know I'm all about the margin! It was off the beaten track, but it worked. Like Mam, I paid ten pounds to hire the hall.

I decided the exercise market could withstand a little bump in retail prices, as some time had passed since Mam's £2.50 sessions all those years before, so I decided to ease it up to three quid, and in no time I'd filled my class! I just followed her model.

I rang all my friends, got them all to come along and bring their Mams, Sisters, Aunties, and friends. Just like Mam, I printed my own flyers, and went posting them all over the area. Suddenly the six o'clock Tuesday slot was full, and I was clearing about £35 profit every time. Considering that I was being paid £3.85 an hour in the café bar, and making ten times that for an hour of exercise (which I loved anyway), it was a small fortune!

Once I'd filled Tuesday, the next logical step was to open another class, which I did on Thursdays in the same place. Soon that class was doing really well too, and I realized I had a choice to make; probably my first big business decision. It was soon going to be time to leave the café bar in order to launch myself into the uncertainty of my own business, and to give it the energy and focus that would make me successful.

The following few weeks were frantic. I worked on building up my timetable of classes and getting additional slots elsewhere, either in health clubs, or setting up more of my own. I'd had fabulous training; Mam was really good at selling things, but she was simply the best at retaining customers. I made it my mission to find out everyone's names, and to always greet them warmly and personally by using their first names. I deliberately made personal contact with them; shaking their hand; a high five; give them a hug; whatever it took to become engaged.

I really tried to create a fitness family. These days it's called your *Third Place*, popularized by Starbucks. You're either at home, at work, or in your Third Place, and once I understood the meaning of this, that's what I endeavoured to give them. In terms of retention, I was trying to deliver a truly personal service, and I kept in touch with everyone between classes. I was also capturing their data in a more sophisticated way than Mam had been able to do with her people. Nowadays I use data capture on my own websites, and AWeber to manage the lists I create, but back then I was collecting names and phone numbers on index cards, and checking them regularly, so that if they suddenly fell off the radar I'd know straight away and I could find them and bring them back.

After a few months of teaching multiple classes every week, I decided to have another go at getting into the Club. I was coming to the end of my notice period in the café bar, and maybe I was worried that I'd lose touch with the Club if I just went off and expanded elsewhere, and I'd never get back. I really saw myself teaching there. It was so nice, so modern, and it suited my aspirations. I'd got myself some experience, so I went along and accosted Dionne once again. I told her what I'd been doing and pleaded for a class.

Once again, she said she thought I was still too young. By this stage I was wondering what I would ever have to do to prove myself. Sure, the first time I'd asked, I'd had nothing to offer. The second time, maybe I was still a little young, but I had the qualification, and I was bounced for lack of experience. But no! In my mind I had ticked all the boxes, and I was gutted that I'd hit the wall again.

And then it happened. One night, she was really stuck for a cover instructor. Somebody had called in sick. It was one of my last shifts in the café bar, and I was just hanging around. Dionne found me and said "Katie, I'm really stuck: can you cover this class?"

What is it they say? Location, Location, Location?

Of course I leapt at the chance. I had ten minutes to put on my gear and plan a class, one I'd never taught before. It was a blur, but I went into the studio, did it, and got really good feedback from the members. We were off and running.

Soon I was covering more classes at the Club, and I'd found my way to the top of the list whenever someone didn't turn up. I made sure that I was always available so that I built a reputation for reliability and consistency. Soon, I got my own weekly class for the first time, and my portfolio started to build. I fitted my outside work and inside work around each other. I had 25 classes a week by the time I was nineteen years old.

I was killing it. I had a beautiful red Mini Cooper Convertible, the business! I was ecstatic. My persistence had eventually paid off, and the only way was up, or so I thought.

But there was a problem; I was rapidly destroying my body by teaching 25 hour-long classes a week. I was picking up injuries, I felt run down and tired, I couldn't get enough sleep, and I realized then that something had to change.

****

Whilst I'd been teaching classes in the studio, I'd always kept an eye on the gym, and I'd observed that the personal trainers who were working in there were able to provide a good service, a personal service, and could still deliver the health and fitness message and help people, but without having to punish their bodies throughout their sessions. They commanded a great hourly rate, but they weren't putting their bodies through it like I was. They were taking a more coaching, supportive role, and they didn't have to physically engage in every bit of the activity they were involved in. The client did the hard work; the Trainer simply demonstrated the exercise, and then coached from the side-lines.

So with one eye on them and one eye on the studio, it looked like an obvious solution for me.

Once again, timing was everything. Dad asked me what I'd like for my 20th birthday. I asked him if I could have a Personal Trainer qualification, and he agreed to pay for it; about £1800!

Once I had my PT qualification, I started to reduce the number of classes I was teaching and increase the amount of personal training hours instead. Because I'd developed a really good client base and personal relationships with hundreds of people, I found that it was really easy to migrate clients from my classes over to my personal training; a natural progression. I was making £35 an hour, without all the set-up and breakdown drama of a church-hall exercise class. But most of all, I was staying fit without hurting myself, so my off-duty life was a lot more relaxed and comfortable.

Within two years, I was the busiest Personal Trainer at the Club. I didn't really have to use any sales strategies. Word-of-mouth referrals were my biggest marketing tool. Everything was working like a charm, and before long I was in a position to buy my first property. I had my nice new car, my new flat, and all the graphs were pointing upwards. I was twenty-three.

Then, without warning, something happened that forced me to realize my business model was totally flawed. All I was doing was exchanging my time for money, and if I didn't have the currency of time to trade, the money would soon dry up.

And as sure as the sunrise in the morning, my currency was about to run out. I was pregnant.

3 - The Romance of... Tesco!

"I was so busy trying to ensure my freedom, I'd created myself a job"

Of course, getting pregnant didn't happen by magic! Despite all the classes, clients, and new business schemes, I had somehow managed to find time for a personal life, too! And that was all about Simon.

Let's backtrack a couple of years. I was twenty-two. I had my business, I was teaching my classes and I was developing my Personal Training client-base at Sunderland Health & Racquets Club. Simon was a member. I used to chat to everybody and I always used to say *Hi* to him, and he always used to say *Hi* to me. One day he just came up to me, completely out of the blue, and asked for some advice.

He'd taken up running; not outside much, but mainly on the treadmill in the gym. Like many people experience when they change their exercise routine or start running for the first time as an adult, he'd had a bit of a twang in his hamstring, which everybody knows is a serious hazard for sport and exercise, and can put you out of action for ages in the most frustrating way. For many people, a tight hamstring feels completely normal until you try to run, when it simply doesn't work properly. And it can take weeks to heal unless you have access to intensive therapy like the professional sports stars, and which most of us simply don't.

I showed him how to use a foam roller and other things that he could do to help alleviate his niggle. We carried on chatting from time to time until one day. I was just clearing up after a class, putting everything back in place in the gym, and he found me.

"Are you going out at the weekend, Katie?"

I told him that I didn't really go out drinking and that kind of thing.

" So do you fancy playing out?" he asked.

"Playing out? What do you mean?" It was a new one on me, or at least I hadn't heard 'playing out' since junior school!

"Do you want to play out at the weekend?" he repeated. I looked at him quizzically.

"I'll tell you what; I'll pick you up on Sunday and we'll go bowling. And if it goes well at the bowling, we'll go to the pictures afterwards. And if that goes well, I'll come to yours for me tea!"

I was speechless, and a little taken aback that someone could be quite that forward, but nonetheless it was quite impressive. It was also kind of silly.

In the end, we agreed on a plan for the following Sunday, but on the Friday, he sent me a message asking, "Are you up to much tonight?"

I replied that (actually) I had no food in at all, and that I needed to go shopping. He came back with another direct proposal; he would pick me up at 7.15 and we'd go food shopping together! Everybody needs food, I suppose!

I panicked. Our first date was to be at the supermarket. How romantic.

He duly picked me up at 7.15, and off we went to the big Tesco Superstore in Durham. We arrived, grabbed our trollies and headed inside. They say you can learn a lot about someone (in this case, a prospective life-partner) by the contents of their shopping trolley. The thing I remember most about that first time shopping with Simon was that he bought Cheese Strings. As you can imagine, to a fitness professional, almost anything that comes in a re-sealable plastic pack is questionable; I just looked at him, looked at the pack, and remarked, "Euw, Processed Cheese!" He's never let me forget it.

Anyway, we somehow managed to get past the processed cheese and find a middle ground on diet and nutrition. Fast-forward eighteen months; we'd moved in together and everything was going great. One day he asked, "Katie, do you fancy a trip through to that big Tesco's at Durham?"

I agreed, and off we went. On the drive over, he started banging on about how much he needed the toilet. When we got to the store, I grabbed the trolley and sent him off to find the lavatory. He was gone for ages, so I started wandering through the store, picking the shopping. He soon found me.

Suddenly, over the Tannoy came an announcement; "Could Katie Bulmer please come to Customer Services?"

I looked at Simon. "Did they just say my name?"

"They did," he said, "you'd better go!"

They were still calling my name. I thought maybe I'd dropped my bank card or something like that. I left Simon with the shopping and hurried across to the service desk. I identified myself to the woman behind the desk, and she gave me a huge smile. Right then I felt a tap on my shoulder, and as I turned, there was Simon, down on one knee with a ring, in the entrance to the store, with the entire staff standing behind him, taking pictures and applauding.

That's how we got engaged, in the middle of Tesco's superstore, Durham branch.

****

So, I was pregnant.

I'd like to say I freaked out, but ever the practical one, my first thought was how on earth I was going to be able to deliver all these classes, sessions, and services and look after a baby as well!

I had to come up with some kind of solution that would help me keep a hold of all my customers and continue to serve them properly, but also give me enough time to do what I had to do. That was when the Little Black Dress Club happened.

Little Black Dress Club is a 6-week, small group Personal Training model, based on the principle that every woman has a little black dress hanging in the back of her wardrobe, which she'd really like to be able to wear again. She felt amazing when she used to wear it, and if she could wear it again, she'd feel amazing again.

I launched the program quickly, and it ran successfully in the local area for around six months. I knew my customer profile; they were female, typically aged 25-55, and what was really great about it was that I could train six people in one session, rather than just one at a time, as with conventional personal training, which really freed-up a lot of my time. But, most importantly, I could still lead my groups despite my rapidly changing body.

I was able to deliver the same package to PT, all the elements of exercise, goal setting, nutrition and support, but it had all the things about group fitness that I loved; the camaraderie, the accountability, the motivation aspects were all there. It was essentially a hybrid of my two disciplines.

After the initial success, I started to think that there must be other ways that I could leverage my time better, and there must also be other fitness professionals in my situation; energy-rich but time-poor. Maybe they had family commitments or a full time job, and were having to fit fitness around it, or just that they were really busy.

So I packaged up what I had been delivering personally to my groups, with the idea to license the program to other trainers across the UK. I knew that it wouldn't be easy, and that what I had to do first was to build up a list of people that I could market it to.

So I started using Social Media campaigns to drive other fitness professionals to my website, to join a mailing list. I gave them regular content at the same time, on the same day, every week. Useful bits and pieces that they could take and adapt for their own fitness businesses and clients. I instinctively knew that going off half-cocked to a crowd of strangers wouldn't work very well, so I put all my spare energy into developing strong relationships and giving useful information for free.

After a few months of building my tribe this way, I felt it was time to try to sell my concept as a licensed product. I put together a webinar and called it *'Why Small Group Training Is The Future Of Fitness'*. Now I am definitely not claiming to have invented anything radical here, however it was very new at the time, and still is, in the fitness industry.

Nearly a hundred people showed up online for the first webinar! I got myself prepared, turned on the machine, and *Showtime!* I used the opportunity to give away some really powerful content, because I needed to prove my credentials and I knew I only had one shot at this audience.

I needed to show them that I knew what I was

talking about. In essence, I gave them everything they needed to take away and start a small-group training program of their own. But at the end of the webinar I told them, "Take it, run with it, do what you want with it, and I wish you the best of luck setting up your own offer. However, if you like what you've heard tonight, and you'd prefer to have the whole thing done for you (there's a method that, you know, really works), then here's the deal..." I had the upsell all worked out.

I offered it to everyone, and on that first event I managed to sign up eleven licenses. I sold it for £347 per license for the initial three months, and then everyone paid £39 a month thereafter. Each month they would receive new content for their clients; new workouts, new marketing strategies, webinars, recipes; all content that they could use directly with their clients, or alternately to drive their own Little Black Dress Club operation forward.

I held a second webinar shortly afterwards, and sold some more licenses. The momentum was building. After a little while I didn't need to hold the webinars any more, because people were coming directly to me by word of mouth, and enquiring about licensing the program. They were seeing how well my licensees were doing with the program, and they wanted in. I had another success on my hands. I really loved doing it.

I ran Little Black Dress Club successfully for two and a half years, and sold licenses to dozens of fitness professionals, both in the UK and abroad. On the back of the Club's success, I won *UK Personal Trainer of the Year*, and *Sunderland Young Business Person of the Year* in the same year, 2012. These awards have done great things for my business, and deserve a chapter of their own. Co-incidentally (with hindsight), the business award was presented to me by the notorious *Apprentice* contestant Katie Hopkins, everybody's favourite flavour of Marmite! Maybe that was a seed being planted.

People have often asked me why I don't own a permanent fitness facility, or a studio or gym. It's simple; that's not my idea of success. It might work for other people, but it wouldn't work for me, because for me, my goal and my measure of my own success are different. My ambitions in business have always been freedom over money, but the Little Black Dress Club was starting to threaten all that.

What I had unwittingly created with the Little Black Dress Club was an administrative overhead for myself, in order to deliver all the elements of the franchise on a tight and rigid schedule. I was still really passionate about what I was doing; I loved it and I had great people working with me, but I felt tied down and restricted by it.

I had created for myself the very thing I'd tried so hard to avoid: *A Job.*

4 - The Fit Mummy Manual.

One of the big lessons that was really brought home to me by my subsequent experience on The Apprentice, and which I was determined to fix when I came home, was that I simply didn't want a job any more. Once again, it was time for my business model to change up.

The way I had set up the Little Black Dress Club, as a license opportunity requiring my constant curation, was sucking time that I needed to utilise for other things if I was going to achieve the business growth I had in mind for myself.

The solution was at hand: I now repackaged it and started to sell it as a Business in a Box. By changing the model, I've been able to maintain a reliable revenue stream, whilst still having pride in a product that is helping fitness professionals deliver a more effective service and build a more successful business. And it still spreads the message of health and fitness, which underpins everything that I do.

I boxed it up and sold it through my website. I still run it, and it continues to be very successful. The people who have bought it have seen great success with it, too, not only from a business point of view (because like me they are better able to leverage their time) but they also report great results for their clients.

By this time I'd become obsessed with the idea of being free; for me, having premises and staff just isn't my bag. I've never wanted to be tied to fixed working hours, so with the goal of total freedom in mind, and also having just become a mother, I now identified a totally new client base; new mothers who wanted to get back in shape after having a baby.

Lots of people were following me on social media. They were watching how I was planning to get back in shape after the birth. I was very open about how I did it, and the challenges I faced, the bits I found easy and difficult. People were showing lots of genuine interest.

But I also felt under immense pressure, because of the position I occupied in the fitness industry, particularly the niche I was in, to get there quickly. I knew that having set out my stall, I now needed to deliver on the promises, and just ten weeks after having Heidi I was back in my skinny jeans, back to where I was physically in terms of aesthetics, but definitely not in terms of my fitness. I didn't have the time to put the gym hours in; I had to take a different approach.

I realised that I didn't have to do anything *extra* to create the collateral for the process. I just needed to log everything. I documented my workouts, I recorded everything I ate and drank, so I'd created all this content in the background, almost as a by-product of my own pre/post-natal process. People were asking, "Katie, how did you do this, I want to do the same," and I realised there was a business in it.

Around this time, I met a girl called Kelly Rennie. I'd been doing some work with her partner Paul for his fitness company. She'd had her baby, Nevaeh, about two or three months earlier, and we got chatting as new Mums do. I discovered that she'd also been keeping track of how she got back into shape because she's a fitness model, and she'd also felt the pressure to get her body back quickly. Just like me, a lot of people had watched what she was doing.

So there we were; she was a model, I was fitness professional, and we'd both felt the same thing. We got to talking about the whole process, in particular, the pressure that we identified as a common factor between us. We talked about breast-feeding, weaning, all the crazy things that you have to do when you first become a new mum; stuff you suddenly become hugely interested in when you have a baby. At the end of the conversation we decided to meet up, which we did in Ripon, half way between her location in Sheffield and me in Sunderland. We wanted to see if there was a way that we could work together and build something useful out of our common experience.

So we went along to the meeting, both of us with our Mothers in tow, so we had somebody to look after the babies whilst we got down to planning our world domination! We looked at the assets we had, which for both of us was a complete log of everything that had happened to us during the process. We were soon convinced that there was a business in it.

From that first meeting, we set about creating *Fit Mummy Manual*. We both wanted the same thing from it; to help other people who'd been in our shoes. The core concept was to help them do it without the pressure that we'd felt. It was clear that women in this situation were being influenced by what was going on in the celebrity world. They were seeing Kim Kardashian and Jennifer Lopez, even the likes of Kerry Katona and Katie Price, pinging back into shape within a few weeks of giving birth. This was giving Mrs. Normal a massive complex; "Why can't I do it?"

The answers were clear to us. It was because we lead different kind of lives. Unlike the celebs, we simply don't have chefs, trainers, and childcare on demand. We really wanted to help the average new mother with all her challenges of time and resources, to do it in a really down-to-earth way. We knew our target customer, because we *were* our target customer. We knew how to do it, and we also knew how hard it was to do, but we had a formula.

In terms of business we both wanted the same thing for ourselves, which was freedom. But we both knew that with babies to look after, we couldn't commit to something that would take up huge amounts of time. So we decided that we'd start a business to market our experience and plan, but that it would be a sideline for us both whilst we continued our day jobs; Kelly as a fitness model, and me as a personal trainer.

We'd do it on the side. So off we went.

The first product we created was *The Fit Mummy Manual* e-book. It brought together the things we had both learned from our own experiences: sensible and results-driven family-oriented nutrition; exercise routines that would occupy no longer than 24 minutes a day, which could be broken down into two twelve-minute sessions without the requirement for a gym, and that only needed you to be in the house next to your baby, without any fancy equipment. Most importantly, we concentrated on instilling a particular mindset, to get people to commit to a process, setting goals, and helping them to stick to their motivation alongside the nutrition and exercise elements.

We pulled it all together into the e-book, did a photo shoot to demonstrate the exercises, and the front cover. But, most importantly, whilst we were creating the product in the background, we were also hard at work building a new e-mail list, and by the time we launched the product, four or five months after our original meeting, we had over two thousand people on that list. And not just anyone, but the *right* audience.

We ran a pre-sale, which went really well, and then we launched the product. *The Fit Mummy Manual* has subsequently sold thousands of downloads. We did next to no advertising, mainly just direct marketing to our list. Kelly's speciality is Facebook ads, and I'm pretty good at writing copy for e-mail marketing, so between us we had the basic skills to get it off the ground.

Initially, the only sales channel was to download the book direct from our website. Later we published the e-book on Amazon Kindle, but in the early days we were selling it for £37 a copy, which served to demonstrate what can be achieved in a really tight, focused, online niche.

Clearly it was popular and we had a hit on our hands. If I had to identify the key factor for our success, apart from the product quality, it was the effort we put into building the list, which we painstakingly did through hands-on social media.

I reasoned that we needed a follow-up product to leverage the interest we had created, and also we were getting a lot of feedback that although the product was good, it was difficult for some of our clients to grasp the exercises from the photographs in the book. So we decided to make a video and distribute in on DVD. It was very simple; we used 6-minute workouts which people could either repeat, or link together to make longer sessions, specifically for new mothers. Along the way, we'd both picked up qualifications as pre- and post-natal exercise specialists, and whatever we were doing, our customers seemed to love it, and bought in their hundreds.

We also needed to keep our expenses low as we'd started the business with no capital, so rather than waste money on plastic cases for the DVD, we simply put them in printed-paper sleeves. Based on the e-book downloads, we'd observed that the US market was very interested in what we were offering. In fact, we'd sold as many books in the US as we had in the UK, so we wanted to keep the DVD shipping costs down, hence the use of sleeves rather than jewel-boxes. We used the same mailing list as we had for the e-book, and the DVD started to perform really well for us.

Next, we started stocking the pink resistance bands that had featured in the exercise routines in the book. Up to that point, we'd been unconsciously promoting other peoples' products for free. We knew from our customer feedback that people who were buying our product for the system then had to go elsewhere for the equipment, and we were missing out on that revenue. So we started selling the bands, and those took off, too! Then we commissioned Fit Mummy workout vests, which sold out immediately.

Next, we decided to try to get into the pre-natal market – exercise during pregnancy – so we created four new workout videos that people could download to their smartphones, depending on which stage of their pregnancy they were in. Based on the earlier success I'd had with another e-book for the Little Black Dress Club, we decided to do a new e-book for nutrition. We'd been getting a lot of questions from new mums about the kinds of food they could eat during breast feeding; largely because of the amount of conflicting and confusing information – much of it old wives tales – that's out there. So our next product was a breast-feeding cookbook, which has ended up being one of our best sellers. We now bundle our products into combination packages, providing a complete pre- and post-natal support system for new Mums.

Clearly there was a good deal of legwork going into this business by now. I've never been particularly keen on outsourcing, partly because of the necessity to keep start-up costs as low as possible, but also because I have an inherent need to control everything at first hand. We didn't want to spend money on websites, so we managed it ourselves. Remember, in the beginning we'd conceived this business as a sideline.

It seemed that whatever we did, our loyal customer base wanted it, so next we installed a members section on the website, and to support that we built an eight-week program that people could follow, with full online support. It did start to impact on our freedom a little, but because it was a high-end product, the revenues (£87 per product) made up for it. We manage it through a Facebook group. So from one basic idea we were quickly able to develop a complete range of products and services, based almost entirely on the feedback we were getting from our customer base. To my mind, it's all about that first early lesson I learned from Mam's exercise classes in the dusty church hall in Sunderland; you don't need a massive global customer base to be successful, just a deep and empathetic understanding of what your target customer is looking for, and a tailored product range to fulfil it.

I've been surprised and amazed at the reach we achieved with the Fit Mummy concept; we have members and subscribers all over the world, and we ship a significant percentage of our products outside the UK, to the USA, Canada, South Africa, Australia, and New Zealand, to mention just a few.

Fit Mummy has far exceeded my initial expectations, and it's grown to be a substantial part of my overall business, having started out as 'a bit on the side'. At the beginning, it was intended to be a pocket-money business, but it's now expanded way beyond that, and continues to grow organically every month. It's turned into a pleasant little monster.

We now use a professional production outfit for the product videos, though we continue to shoot our own promotional stuff ourselves on our iPhones. The people that follow us seem to like the fact that we are down to earth and can identify with our audience. Like them, we have busy lives to run. Kelly's had another baby, which was great for business, although I'm not tempted myself at this stage. There's too much to do; we are the Fit Mummies!

Even now, we take care of all the fulfillment ourselves. We pack and mail out the products, manage our website and social feeds, and handle all our customer service. Operationally, nothing is outsourced. The control freak in me demands it! I want to know exactly what's going on with my business in real time.

The big message is this; if you have a good idea,

you can start a business without any money, simply by committing a little time to learning how to do stuff yourself. It'll save you a fortune down the road.

Now we needed to expand and make more sales. We needed PR. That's when I had a big idea that would change everything...

5 - The Princess and the PR

It was New Year 2013. I wanted to get *the Fit Mummy Manual* brand out there and for it to be massive, but I didn't have a big marketing budget (or even a small one come to that!) Even if I could have afforded it, I didn't want to put it in the hands of a marketing and PR agency. I wanted to do it myself, but I'm not (wasn't) a marketer, and I'm not an expert in PR. What I needed was a game-changer.

I was sitting at my desk one day, wondering how I could get some good publicity without spending any money. I can't remember what triggered it, but suddenly I had an idea - Royal Endorsement!

The hottest news at the time was the impending arrival of Prince George, the royal baby, son and heir to Prince William and Kate Middleton, the Duchess of Cambridge. I Googled *Clarence House*, got the address, grabbed a Fit Mummy DVD and a jiffy bag, and packaged it up with a little letter. I took it down to the post office, thinking, *"I've got nothing to lose, and fortune favours the brave!"*

What was the worst that could happen? The DVD and packaging cost less than a pound! So sent it off, not knowing whether anything would come of it. To my complete surprise and shock, a couple of weeks later I got a letter back from St James' Palace, written on beautiful parchment with the royal seal on the envelope and an embossed logo at the top, from Rebecca, Kate Middleton's assistant, thanking me for sending *The Fit Mummy Manual* DVD. I couldn't believe it.

ST JAMES'S PALACE

From   Miss Rebecca Deacon
Private Secretary to HRH The Duchess of Cambridge

Private and Confidential

18th January, 2013

Dear Katie and Kelly (if I may),

The Duchess of Cambridge has asked me to write and thank you for your letter of 12th December, in which you make Her Royal Highness aware of the services you provide as pre and post natal exercise specialists.

It was extremely kind of you to take the trouble to write as you did, and The Duchess would have me send you her warmest thanks and best wishes.

Yours sincerely,

Rebecca Deacon

Ms. Katie Bulmer-Cooke and Ms. Kelly Rennie,
The Fit Mummy Manual

But then I started to wonder what I could do with it?

My first action was to call the local paper, The Sunderland Echo, and the local radio station, and managed to get myself on the air, telling them that Kate had a copy of my DVD and that I had the letter to prove it. The next thing I knew, the national press had picked it up and I was being asked to do a whole bunch of interviews. Then I found out that on the other side of the world, the Australian and New Zealand press had also got hold of the story, and it was all over their women's magazines, too! Of course, out in the Commonwealth, anything to do with the royal baby was huge news! The story made it into women's magazines all around the world. I had my game-changer!

As I've mentioned over and over, I'm not a great believer in outsourcing, especially when I can learn how to do things for myself. With the Princess and the PR, if I had outsourced my marketing, who's to say that my agency would ever have had that idea, and that they'd have been able to turn it around so quickly? For sure it would have cost a lot more than the one single pound I'd invested in the whole thing!

I'd also been told that I should outsource my web design; that somebody else should always take care of the stuff that isn't your speciality. If I had done that, and had wanted to put this amazing news highlight live on my site, with the *"as used by the*

Duchess of Cambridge" tag line, I would have had to send all the material to the web designer, then wait for them to do the formatting and the upload. Knowing how fast the Internet moves, particularly social media feeds, the impact would have been over by the time the message got out. I had taken the time, early in the piece, to teach myself some simple coding and Wordpress design techniques. I had my letter from the palace, and I was able to put the whole thing up online instantly.

Don't get me wrong; I do understand that my way is not the only way, and although it's right for me and the way I like to run things, it might not be right for every small business. But since I've always understood the instantaneous nature of the communication channels that work best for me, I had no choice but to do the important stuff myself if I wanted to be moving at the same speed as the rest of the online world.

It's just a question of turnaround time. On Twitter, I know how to use the correct hashtags to get noticed, how to make journalists aware. In the hands of outsourced agencies, I might have missed the opportunity. As it was, I managed to make this little piece of news both fresh and current, up to the minute, and not allow somebody else to have control of my business. I always want to stay in the driving seat.

Another thing that's always made me nervous about outsourcing online marketing and media is the potential for roadblocks. For example, if you fall out with your freelancers or agencies, they hold the keys to the castle, and if they decide to play rough you can be out of business in a very short time indeed. They have all the passwords, hosting, domain access, everything, which could be potentially catastrophic. To me it's important that I can make instant changes in my business, and without relying on someone else's interpretation or availability.

And what an opportunity it was. From that one simple initiative and the luck of it getting picked up by the media, things really started to change for *The Fit Mummy Manual*. Up until then we'd be shipping steadily to clients in the UK, but on the back of this publicity we started to see traffic from all over the world; suddenly our little part-time project was global.

On the back of the royal 'connection', America started to become interested in what we were doing, and we now have more customers in the USA than our home market. We also picked up customers in Australia, New Zealand, Japan, Mexico, France, Canada, and other places, too. The US thing has been interesting for us. We'd always defined ourselves as a British product for a largely British market, but now we were finding that the Americans loved what we were doing, too.

It was the game changer.

Now we needed to fill our pipeline with new products, to leverage this wave of eager new customers that we were attracting. Remember, for this business the target demographic was clearly defined. Unless you were pregnant or recently post-natal, you wouldn't have any interest in what we were selling, so the logical step was to stay firmly in our Fit Mummy comfort zone, and build other products and services to fulfil the demand for more.

Next we created an 8-week online Fit-Mummy transformation programme. Kelly and I figured out how to install a program called 'Wish-list Member' onto our website, so that we could administer, operate, and charge for subscribing members. We set up eight weeks' worth of follow-up content, and I taught myself how to synchronise it with our e-mail database on AWeber. We'd quickly created a solid second product to follow on from the Princess and the PR. Once again, it cost us next to nothing.

The feedback from our customers was consistent. They liked our real-people approach, as an alternative to the glitzy celebrity-mum offerings with which they're constantly bombarded. It demonstrates the immense pressure that women feel to get back into their skinny jeans after childbirth, which the celebrity media pushes down everyone's throats. We were 'keeping it real' and reaching out to people who could identify with us as people, as well as the advice and guidance we were giving and selling them.

We structured the program to give them an accessible and achievable approach, but one that delivers results, without the airbrushed magazine shots or the fad diets. I find it enormously rewarding, because that's precisely what we'd set out to achieve. We get a lot of feedback telling us that people are really benefitting from what we offer, which is great to hear and makes the whole thing so worthwhile.

I still find it amazing to believe that a lady in Mexico is popping our DVD in her machine, and we're popping up on her screen. It's surreal, but it goes to demonstrate the global nature of this time we live in, and how you can reach the whole world from a back bedroom in Sunderland!

We get all our initial sales via social media campaigns, and we've worked hard on building a great organic following on Twitter. These are the right people. They stay with us because we feed them interesting, useful content on a regular basis. That builds trust, which is an especially important aspect of social media. Once we have the first sale, and the e-mail marketing cuts in, this gives us a two-way direct channel of communication which is hard to achieve on social media alone. We're able to keep in touch with our customers, and remain consistent. We do lots of offers and promotions, which we see as a way of saying thanks to our customers for their initial purchase. The underlying message is clear; *now that you're on our list, we are going to look after you properly.* Direct marketing covers a broad spectrum of emotions for people, and many companies and businesses don't pay enough attention to the trust and integrity aspects, which we always keep front and centre in all our communications.

Lately we started to use Instagram, and we've found that we get lots of engagement and interaction from our followers on that platform. People are decreasingly interested in reading text bulletins, and are beginning to respond much more enthusiastically to pictures, which is what Instagram is all about. Time is the most valuable commodity nowadays, and they want to see a picture and no more than one short, punchy paragraph, or they can easily switch off and move onto the next thing. We've also applied what we learned on Instagram to our e-mail marketing. I predict Instagram will be massive in the future, especially for businesses like ours.

Of course we tweet daily, so as not to be intrusive. With Facebook, my business partner Kelly is the expert in our team. She understands how to optimise the advertisements so that they reach the right audiences at the right time, and she understands how to piggyback onto other trends in our sector, such as people searching for baby clothes and prams, rather than purely the fitness angle. I call it "guilt by association," and that works great.

Our latest development is a smartphone app that also distributes all the free content that we've given out over the past few years. It's easy and quick, and rather than facing the challenge of getting recipients to open our e-mails, with our app we can send push messages directly to users' screens, so they see our stuff automatically. We push out a few messages each week, and it drives additional sales, because they can shop directly from the app.

The lesson is clear: Social Media is a fantastic promotional opportunity for small business, but you need to focus on the channels which are most suited to your sector, and learn how to use them properly. The objective is to create a funnel, and drive people towards a direct communication channel, in our case e-mail, and then use an empathetic and community approach to turn your tribe into real customers.

6 - The Apprentice

I applied online for the Apprentice late in 2013, and really didn't think much about it; in fact I pretty much forgot over Christmas. I knew that a lot of people would apply, and I didn't know if I stood a chance. But I realised I had nothing to lose by putting myself out there; what's the worst that could happen? Perhaps I wouldn't get any further in the process. Then out of the blue, just after New Year I received an e-mail from the BBC asking me to come to the first round of auditions in Manchester.

That woke me up!

I was really nervous because I knew it would be full of interviews and pressure, and I was apprehensive because someone else would be in the driving seat. Having worked for myself since the very beginning, I'd never had a job interview, so the reason that I was so nervous was because I knew that the control would be taken away from me, and would be facing an interview panel.

I had no idea what to expect, which was a totally alien sensation for me; fear of the unknown. For a moment I regretted ever getting involved in the first place, but then the excitement of a new challenge took over. I knew that it could be a massive opportunity for me, and if I wanted it, I would have to step right outside my comfort zone.

So on the 24th January, I swapped my trainers and leggings for smart, flat shoes (never heels), tights and a black dress, which was a real dress-up day for me, and headed off nervously to Manchester. All the way there, I was thinking about turning back; *did I really need this kind of pressure?*

I arrived, stomach in knots, at the Radisson Blu Hotel, where the selection process was taking place. I was shown into a cavernous function room with loads of chairs scattered around. I nervously handed over the information they'd asked me to bring.

In the room, there were around forty other people. The guys were in sharp suits, and the girls were all dressed up to the nines, in designer dresses with six-inch heels, big bouncy hair, all looking gorgeous and glamorous, and there was me, the only girl in flats, in my Top Shop dress, short hair, and feeling well out of place!

I felt thoroughly intimidated, and I was sitting there thinking to myself, *"Katie, what HAVE you done?"* I sat there for what seemed like an age, when one of the production team called my name, along with nine others, and we were led in silence to another room. On the floor were ten places, marked with numbered cards, and we were told to take our positions. I was number eight.

In front of us was a small table with two interviewers from the production team. We were then told that they would call our numbers at random, at which point we were each to step forward and would have thirty seconds to sell ourselves. No preparation. I was totally stressed about the situation I found myself in, and I really didn't feel like I had any way out.

The first number called was number two; at least I wasn't going first! This young, nondescript guy stepped forward and spoke very passionately for his thirty seconds, about his love for recruitment consultancy, how he felt that he would be the right person for the process, that he was sure he could win and that he had a dynamite proposition for Lord Sugar. To be honest, as passionately as he might have felt that he spoke, to me he was plain vanilla; nothing exciting about him whatsoever. But I also thought, to be fair to him, he had gone first, which I would definitely not have wanted, so as he stepped back to his mark at the end of his pitch, without thinking about it I automatically started to applaud him, loudly and enthusiastically. That's just my nature; if I think someone's done a good job, I'll always show my appreciation.

What I soon realised was that as I was applauding the guy, the rest of the room was silent! I was the only one clapping, and everyone else in the room was looking at me! Gradually my clapping started to slow down, as the interviewers fixed me with their steely glare, and I was still clapping, slower all the time. In my head I was screaming in panic, "*So we don't need to clap?*" They clearly understood my panic state, and mimed back a kind of "*no!*"

OK, so I don't need to clap.

I don't remember anything about what happened in my thirty seconds. I can't even remember what I said. It was so pressurised, and I was operating on autopilot by then. The rest of the session was and remains a complete blur. However, I was one of five who were told to go to the next stage of the process. But what I did take from the situation was that, even though I can't remember what I said, I had done something different from my competition. And they *were* my competition, even at that early stage.

I didn't perhaps dazzle the production team with a strong, wordy explanation of what I did, but I obviously stood out by doing the opposite to my opponents. Bringing that into a business scenario, throughout my career, whenever I've read a business guru's book or followed someone on a blog, even down to what I learned in the business modules that I studied in my university years, I was always told to assess the competition, then do one of two things; do the same as them but do it better, or alternately do exactly what they do, but do it cheaper. But for me, despite that repetitive advice, what I've learned in my business career, and what that first experience at the Apprentice underlines is that if the competition do one thing, then often the best thing to do is go in the other direction.

In that case, the others were all giving well-rehearsed and articulate speeches in the audition process, and there's nothing intrinsically wrong with that if it suits one's personality. Meanwhile, I was standing there clapping and applauding, at the other extreme. That made me stand out that day, and it got me through to the next stage. On such relatively small and insignificant events, situations can turn, and in that case, and in all my business experiences before and since, that *'zig when they zag'* philosophy has worked pretty well for me.

I always try to stand out from the crowd. When I conceived *The Fit Mummy Manual,* there was nothing else like it on the market, even though the marketplace itself was extremely crowded with products and services chasing the same customer for the same reason. It was all a bit too frumpy and inaccessible for my liking. Far too airbrushed and celebrity-based, and I wanted to do something different, more basic and down to earth.

Likewise, with the Little Black Dress Club, people told me I would alienate a lot of potential customers by saying that I just wanted to work with a particular niche; to get them back into their little black dress. But for me, it was about standing out and not only creating a niche, but also pulling people toward my product with a specific kind of offer that I instinctively knew would speak to the people I wanted to work with.

That first Apprentice audition was a good summary of what I've always tried to do in business, and what I would recommend that other people consider when trying to find their place in a market.

Obviously, the mystique of the Apprentice is largely based on what people don't know about what goes on off-screen, so I'm limited in what else I can say about it. Far be it from me to spill the beans and give anyone an unfair advantage going into future series, but what I can say is that later on in the process, there were more and longer interviews, which were a major part of the selection process to get down to the final twenty for the televised shows.

The other thing that I recognise from the early part of the Apprentice process was that I had to step well outside my personal comfort zone, and do things that were not only alien to me, but which I had subconsciously avoided in the past. It was really uncomfortable at times, and I think that's a big reason why so many people never actually go after the business that they want, simply because they're afraid that they'll have to do things that they'll hate, or that will scare them. They worry that they'll fail, or about what someone else might think, or even judge them. That's exactly how I felt throughout all the interview stages in the auditions. However, being outside my comfort zone was the only way that I was ever going to be able to progress, and grab the opportunity.

It's ironic that I left the Apprentice process the very week before the infamous *interview round*, when the candidates are taken apart by Lord Sugar's 'trusted advisors'. Some say I dodged a bullet, but actually I would have relished the opportunity to face them all. That was the moment I had been building up to. To have got to that stage would have meant taking my destiny into my own hands, and I knew I could handle it better being told that I was fired because I'd messed up my own pitch, rather than as a part of a team effort that went wrong.

Although I feel now that I'm a really good team player, I've always worked on my own. I'm sometimes surprised at how successful I've managed to be working in partnership with Kelly on the Fit Mummy project, but we are different and complementary. I'm the analytical, strategic one, whilst she tends to be the ideas half of the partnership. Two halves of a whole.

To summarise the lessons: first; do the things that scare you, because once you've done them you add them to the sum total of your competences and experiences, and they won't scare you nearly as much the next time.

Secondly; differentiate yourself from your competition; *zig when they zag!*

However, I was in. And little did I know how my life was about to change!

7 – Two Places At Once!

Going to the Apprentice, of course, meant going away from home. I was worried about leaving my business. In the past, I'd tried bringing other trainers on board, but it never really worked out. Because what I'd always done, and not always deliberately, was to build my business around Me, my personality, and the way I work. I have tried several times to drill down and analyse my business; what do I do, what are my techniques, nutrition plans, and so on, and how to have someone else deliver it all.

It just never quite worked. I guess it may be because the magic ingredient was the relationship I built up with my customers, and I had no way of controlling how other people performed in that area. Starting cold with somebody else was always going to be a challenge. When I sold Little Black Dress Club in a box, that worked very well because I had not worked with those clients in the past. It was an existing person with an existing client base, simply taking on something new, rather than someone trying to fill *my* shoes with *my* customers. So it required a completely different approach.

Obviously, I was nervous about leaving the business, but I did have one fantastic trainer who could fill in for me with my one-on-one and small group sessions, called Laura. She had started out as a client, but she got so into the whole fitness thing that she went off and qualified as a Personal Trainer herself. She had her Level 3 qualification, and she had a great existing relationship with everyone in my group; she knew them all. I'm so grateful for Laura, because I think that had I tried to hand it over to a stranger, I might have come back to a very different business.

Another big lesson that I've learned is this; in the fitness industry, because traditionally we all sell our time for money, when we want a holiday or we have to go sick, it's a nightmare. You lose so much money. If you're spending money on vacations and not earning at the same time, every holiday ends up costing double the price. I know this isn't just an issue for people like me: anyone running a small business, which relies on them being present, is going to suffer the same problem.

It was this challenge that really motivated me to create my online products and services, so that the businesses could run on autopilot if I couldn't be in the office. Had I not set these up in the previous years, I don't know if going to the Apprentice could have been a practical possibility for me. Those businesses were able to tick over as normal, even whilst I was in isolation, which I knew would be one of the main conditions of participating in the show.

People were still able to buy products from the website, and I was completely removed.

Right from the very first e-mail calling me for

the audition, the Apprentice producers were very clear about the filming dates when the candidates would be required. It was a seven-week period. During that time, there would be no home visits; everyone would be completely committed, living in 'the house,' and essentially cut off from the outside world.

It simply serves to underline that modern technology allows business people to set things up automatically. Ten years ago, none of this would have been possible.

So before I left, I scheduled all my newsletters and my sales promotions, using AWeber. I had promotional codes and sales plugged into the IT, and throughout the time that I was away, everything ran smoothly. The whole setup took me less than a day.

I knew the newsletter was critical. For many months, I'd been sending out 'Katie's Wake-Up Call' at the same time on the same day each week, and from the feedback and response it receives, I knew that it had become a central pillar of my relationship management with my customer. It's a little rod for your back, because if you start missing weeks, customers hardly notice, but they do forget about you when they're subconsciously used to seeing something upbeat from you every Monday. It's a trust issue, and I know it leads to the majority of my online sales.

It was a bit of a head-scratcher to try to come up with seven weeks worth of quality content in one session, but I managed it, and once all the schedules were set-up, I knew that I was ready to head off on my Apprentice adventure.

All my social media postings were scheduled, too. Although I'm almost exclusively digital in my business, I still find that a wall planner is the easiest way to get a picture of the weeks and months ahead, spotting public and school holidays, and planning sales promotions and special events so they have the biggest potential audiences and the least possibility of distraction. Things like National Fitness Days are meat and drink to me.

This was also a defining moment for me in the perpetual "Have you got a business or a job?" debate. For me, a business definitely needs to be something that you can leave, and which can run on without you being constantly there. The alternative is just the definition of a job.

Leaving was a big test. What I realised was that there were still some elements of my business that were actually more like a job. One thing's for sure; you'll never really know where you stand on the 'business/job spectrum' until you try leaving it. I was to have no e-mail access and no mobile phone. For all intents and purposes, I was going into outer space for nearly two months. Scary!

I had total trust in Laura to run my client sessions, but it was the online side of the business that I was putting to the test. I didn't know if what I had created was truly generating passive income or if I had taken my job and put it online. In the end, the schedule dictated that I had to be satisfied with the preparations I'd made because there would be no chance to make modifications once the TV rocket blasted off!

So back to the Apprentice interview process. After that first group interview session, five people had been shown the door, and there were five of us left. I had no idea what was coming, which was worrying. I had no idea how many stages there were in the selection process, who I was going to meet next, or what I would be asked to do. For someone who revels in control, this was very unsettling, and put me in touch with a bunch of feelings that I'd never experienced before. It was challenging, but it was also exciting. I'd made it through stage one, and that inspired me with at least a little more confidence.

No one was telling us much, and the whole audition process was shrouded in secrecy, to add to the air of mystery for anyone coming in. They obviously didn't want anything to be given away.

The next phase consisted of a one-to-one interview with one of the production team, to ask you about what you do, and compare the *real you* to the details you had written in your online application. I think anyone who's ever watched the final interview stage in the Apprentice TV shows will know that some of the candidates do tend to over-egg the pudding, and they inevitably get exposed, once someone starts to forensically examine their claims.

When I walked into the room, it was like a speed dating setup, with ten or twelve tables and an interviewer and a candidate sitting opposite each other. I took my seat. It all felt very serious; nobody was laughing or joking. It was intense. My interviewer was a girl a couple of years younger than me, and she had my application forms spread out in front of her. As we chatted through the various bits and pieces, within thirty seconds we started to find some empathy and I had her laughing and giggling! In the whole room, we were the only ones! The interview lasted about ten minutes, and as we came to an end, she said to me, "OK Katie, so the final question; what is twenty percent of fifteen hundred?"

My mind went blank. I just looked at her and asked, "Are you joking?" which clearly she wasn't.

Now, mental arithmetic has never been my strong point so I told her that I could give her an answer if she could provide me with a pen and paper, or a calculator! She thought it was hilarious, but she gave me a pen, and I worked it out.

But just when I thought that was the end, there was a final question; "How do you rate me as an interviewer, out of ten?"

I told her that I would rate her as nine but that I would have given her ten until she'd asked the maths question! In that interview, what stood out for me was the seriousness in the room. I'd had two choices; I could have folded under the maths question, or made light of my limited ability, which is what I did. I guess it worked, and as a result, she asked one of the runners to "Take Katie to the next stage!"

Once again, I had dared to be different. Instinctively, I knew that I wasn't that person who could be so serious and intense, as all the other candidates in the room were being. I just felt that they would be looking for something more, and I instinctively gave them my attempt at being different.

And guess what? I was the only one that made it out of that room. People were leaving, left, right, and centre. Every few moments, people were being shown the way out.

By the end of the day, I was sitting alone in the corridor. I was the only one left. I was looking around thinking *Wow!* Because I'd gone in so nervous and intimidated, from the first moment I'd been convinced I wasn't going to make it through the day. All those talented, glamorous, gregarious young people, in their sharp suits and their high heels. Now here I was, sitting on my own, waiting to go to what I now know to be the final stage of the selection process. Sitting there, by myself, gave me an enormous confidence boost.

The final event of the day was to go into a room and be interviewed on camera, exactly as it would be on the TV show. But those few minutes alone in the corridor gave me time to think about what had happened. Being different had worked well for me. I asked myself why I had worried so much, and reached the only conclusion that I could; that my way was actually the right way. At least on that particular day!

It had been a very pressurised experience, but this final on-camera interview was brutal; they questioned everything; my character, my business sense, and the plan that I was bringing to present to Lord Sugar in the final stages of the TV shows if I was ever going to get that far. But the process itself had empowered me and built up my confidence, without which I think I would have floundered in the final interview.

The message: to find out what you are really capable of, you sometimes have to do the things that scare you the most. You need to be under pressure and on the spot, or you'll never know how you'll react if it comes along unexpectedly.

8 – Look Mam, I'm On The Telly!

Wow! From thousands of applicants I had made it through to the final twenty, to appear on the Apprentice 2014 on BBC One. It was all very real now, and I'd already gone a lot further than I'd ever imagined. Most importantly for me, I'd already learned a huge amount about how to handle competition, and how not to allow myself to be intimidated by others, no matter how shiny and superior they portrayed themselves!

Following the Manchester auditions, the next few weeks were a whirlwind. I'd had two more rounds of auditions in London before I was finally told that I'd been selected (to borrow a phrase from X-Factor) for the Live Shows. At the end of April, I packed my kit and headed off for the process proper, in London.

I had no idea about what I was heading into, other than what I'd seen on TV in previous series of the show. There was no itinerary, and no schedule was provided; it was all about going with the flow.

The first time the candidates were together in one place was just before the first boardroom, where we were to be introduced to Lord Sugar, and his faithful sidekicks, the laconic Nick Hewer and the impressive and razor sharp Karen Brady, exactly as it's shown on TV. We all rocked up in separate cars and gathered in the boardroom reception, but we were instructed that there should be no talking to each other. So we stood in silence, a group of twenty hopefuls (and a few wannabes), waiting for the action to begin.

All I could do was look around, and form impressions based only on how people appeared.

After a little while we were shown into the boardroom itself, to meet the boss of all bosses, Lord Alan Sugar. Of course the purpose, once the cameras started rolling, was for us candidates to meet *him*, not to meet each other, so my impression of the others was rapidly modified by how they pitched themselves, in one of the most intimidating environments most of us had ever experienced.

In case you're unfamiliar with the show; twenty (they'd increased it from sixteen in previous years) young entrepreneurs compete over twelve weeks to become The Apprentice, at which point Lord Sugar invests £250,000 into a joint business venture, based on the plan that the candidates bring with them. The candidates operate as two teams, competing in a variety of business tasks, and being gradually eliminated until the final. It's winner takes all, so everyone knows that it's going to get pretty cut-throat as the process rolls forwards.

In the boardroom, we introduced ourselves in turn, giving a quick description of our business plan, and we were briefed on the first assignment. It was to be a *selling task*, which immediately made me nervous as I've never felt confident in calling myself a salesperson, although I was soon to discover selling was what I'd actually been doing for several years. Perhaps this goes to show that you need to understand what it is that you do that makes your business successful? It might come as quite a surprise to find that you're actually excelling at things that you don't even recognise as part of your skill set!

There I was, surrounded by people who looked like they were all about sales. They looked the part; they talked the talk.

Once the first boardroom ordeal was out of the way, we finally had the chance to meet each other properly. It was in the garden of the huge London town house that we were to be living in for as long as we could cling on to our places. There was free-flowing champagne to help everyone loosen up, though in my case I stuck to orange juice. There's my little control-freak again!

We'd seen each other throughout the day, but we hadn't been allowed to speak until the cameras were rolling, so that they could capture the realistic situation of us all meeting for the first time. In the hours leading up to that first meeting, I'd had the chance to look at all the other people and I had made the mistake that everyone warns you about in life; never judge a book by it's cover. I'd already made assumptions, particularly about the nine women that I now found myself involved with, and some of the boys as well.

At this point, we were split into the original teams, which started out as girls versus boys. We headed off to have our first board meeting for the team, choose a name, and plan how we were going to execute the opening task, the very next day.

For the first time, I was hearing more detailed information about these other women. What I found was that once we started talking, almost every assumption I had made was wildly inaccurate! For example, everyone who watched the show would remember Sarah; tall, blonde, leggy, a formidable woman, or so I thought. She'd strutted into the first boardroom meeting with a really powerful aura, totally intimidating, with amazing posture, and power-dressed in a blue business suit. But when it came to actually talking to her, what came out of her mouth was absolutely nothing like the external impression that I'd formed.

In fact, from what I'd perceived to be a strong and powerful business women, totally switched on, her sales strategy for the first task, for which she was Project Manager, was to be for the girls' team to wear short skirts, plenty of makeup, and red lipstick! I was horrified to the point of seriously questioning my own assumptions about the world of business, in fact the world in general. Maybe she was right? Maybe that was the way the world worked, outside of my cosy little Sunderland fitness enclave! For a moment I really began to doubt myself, and prepared to adjust all my frames of reference, which was worse than confusing!

I'd spent hours building a perception of Sarah, and now here I was discovering the real person, and for a brief moment I was almost ready to buy into whatever she said. But the trigger was the red lipstick suggestion, at which point my sensible side took control. Red lipstick is not something I'd usually wear, not in this life anyway, and that comment alone burst the bubble, and I began to realise that my initial impressions were grossly flawed!

And it wasn't just Sarah. Some of the others were equally as surprising.

Right from the start I'd been worried about going into this process because I knew I didn't have a traditional corporate background. Having been obsessed with fitness and performance since the beginning of my career, I'd never studied business. But I'd loaded up on jargon and buzz-words before I arrived, in order to make sure I wouldn't make a fool of myself until I got the lay of the land, and thinking that all the others on the journey were bound to be more experienced and professional. I'd imagined that everyone else would be so far ahead of me, that I'd be playing constant catch-up, but the truth was very different.

I saw the cracks start to appear straight from the off. Sarah wanted us to dress like tarts to bring in business. Nurun, another of the candidates, told us all that we were *decadent* when she clearly didn't understand the meaning of the word. As these layers of imperfection revealed themselves in the other candidates, my confidence was growing in leaps and bounds. They simply weren't the super humans I'd previously perceived them to be!

When the original teams were assigned, we had to come up with a name for our team. I put forward 'Grafters,' which on reflection probably wouldn't have made it through to the edit; too real, but then that's me. The others turned their back on that idea. I guess that's not how they saw themselves. It wasn't glamorous enough, and sounded a bit too much like getting your hands dirty. To me, that's what business is all about; sheer hard graft. It was clear that very few of those other candidates had ever run any kind of business for themselves. Sure, there were some high-powered wage-slaves there, and no doubt they'd worked very hard to achieve some of their impressive positions (at least based on the resumes they'd submitted with their application) but it was clear to me that very few of them actually understood the demands and effort that goes into a small business like mine. I had found another edge.

By now my confidence was really growing. With every conversation, I was able to measure myself against the other people, and I was beginning to like what I was hearing.

I was really taken aback by the house. It was a bizarre environment, sort of halfway between Through the Keyhole and Big Brother! The place was incredible to look at from the outside, but once inside it was set up like a bunkhouse. When we first arrived, I looked around and noticed that the bedrooms were organised with three or four little beds, almost like military bunks! Now, as an only child and an admitted business loner I wasn't looking forward to sharing anything, especially space, and especially with strangers. The prospect of sleeping with others in the bedroom was daunting enough, but sharing a bathroom?

Luckily for me, I was assigned a room with just two others, Lindsay the swimming teacher and Roisin who made it all the way to the final five. We soon discovered that we actually had quite a lot in common, particularly centred on family and roots. Like me, Roisin was married, and Lindsay had a little daughter, and they were really down-to-earth people, which helped me feel at home. Unpretentious; no airs and graces.

Discovering that I was to be bunking with them was a massive relief. For me, nothing could have been worse than finding out that I would be sharing my space with people who I didn't get on with, or who weren't my cup of tea. I had no problem working with different kinds of people on the tasks, but to then have to go home and sleep with them wasn't really what I'd envisioned. When I think back, I hadn't really considered this aspect of what I had embarked upon, so to find myself with people who I liked was a big bonus.

The first evening was all about unpacking. Of course the TV show would lead you to believe that we all survived for two months on the contents of a little wheelie-bag, because that's what we always took with us when we headed to the boardroom at the end of each task. But you'd need to be a magician to conjure up a new professional look each day, and recycling my smalls is not something I'd really fancy, especially to be on TV, so behind the scenes we all had enormous suitcases full of clothes, and that took most of the first evening to unpack.

We all knew that tomorrow would bring the first task, but it had been such an overwhelming day that we were already exhausted. So when the telephone rang at around 4 a.m. the next morning, nobody got up to answer it! To be fair, none of us even knew what the phone would sound like, and everyone was sleeping soundly, so it just rang and rang until eventually someone from the production crew shouted up the stairs, *"Will one of you answer the bloody phone!"*

I'm told that the phone rang three separate times before someone finally got up and answered it.

What the viewer sees, a bunch of panicking candidates rushing around with bed-head hair, looking like a dog's dinner; that's the real deal. The crew quietly infiltrates the house during the night, and they capture things exactly as they happen.

On the first morning, we were given just twenty minutes to get ready. It was the first time in the history of the show. I'd mentally prepared myself for half an hour, and I knew I could be ready. But twenty minutes? In a flat spin, I managed to wash and dry my hair, which included at least five minutes trying to find my hairdryer, and somehow I managed to make myself look presentable. Goodness knows how some of the other girls managed, with their high demands of make-up, and the red lipstick!

If I'd thought I'd been nervous earlier in the process, this was off the scale. My stomach was doing somersaults and I felt physically sick. I was terrified that I would allow the intimidation of these high-powered people to cause me to retreat into myself. I had form in that department, as Mam had pointed out to me in the past, and it was on my mind. I knew I needed to set out my stall from the beginning.

Week 1: 'Ten Years of Selling'

20 Candidates Begin

All episodes of The Apprentice UK Season 10 are available to view on YouTube.

With the contestants split into girls and boys, the teams set off to sell a variety of everyday items, including (amongst others) sausages and t-shirts...

Soon we were off and running. The first task day was incredibly pressurised, and I was so happy to get back to the house and be in my bedroom with the other two girls, with a shared experience behind us, and the opportunity to relax and be ourselves. They weren't family, but on that day they were as close as it was going to get.

So, in the beginning, the little tribes were formed by the way bedrooms separated us. Up until then, everyone was a stranger, and the first thing we had in common was simply that we shared a room, so it was inevitable that we would gravitate to each other, and form bonds based on that.

But after that first task was over, I thought back, particularly about Sarah, who had scared me the first time I saw her with her power dressing and her ambition to be the first Project Manager, but who had proven almost the opposite once the action began. Although we'd won that first task, she had shown herself to be someone completely different. Once more,

I was feeling strong and confident, and I think I realised that I had as much right to be there as everyone else. What I was seeing was outdated strategy, and many of my preconceptions were removed. I knew then that I could start to position myself higher up the pecking order than my first impressions had suggested.

The other thing that had really changed my perception was the first boardroom firing. When Chiles, the first candidate to lose his seat, had been shown the door, I suddenly realized that this was game-on. It was for real. There was a thoroughly smart, switched on guy who I'd chatted to the previous evening, and he was gone in a flash. If he could leave, anyone could be next, and I knew this was a signal for me to raise my game.

I was on my way.

Week 2: 'Wearable Tech'

19 Contestants Remaining.

With the Girls (Team Decadence) having aced the first task, the Boys (Team Summit) entered the task determined to get even. At Imperial College, Lord Sugar announces that the teams must invent an item of Wearable Technology, which they will then pitch to three leading retailers. Sugar made a strong suggestion that hipster Robert should put himself forward as PM for the Boys Team. However, Robert declined. Scott, a healthcare specialist, takes it on, but it's not a happy camp.

The Girls need a new name. Decadence ditched, Team Tenacity emerges, after Katie makes absolutely sure that everyone understands the definition! Again, there was a lot of ducking and diving, but Katie exerts her influence to persuade Nurun an Asian Fashion Retailer, to take it on.

The boys come up with an idea ("The Emoti Shirt - On Air") to use a T-Shirt that will display a video photograph uploaded from a phone; the Selfie Sweatshirt. The girls decide on a jacket with solar panels in order to be able to power colourful lighting on the lapels and internal heating.

In the design phase, Katie steps up and takes charge, but complications in the design meant the girls suffer a serious delay in production of the prototype. In the pitch, the consensus is that the functions were too elaborate. Meanwhile, the boys are meeting accusations of 'Christmas Jumper'.

Sadly, Nurun's pitch is a disaster.

To the boardroom. On the Boys' side, the refusal of Robert to take on the PM job draws severe criticism from both sides of the table. "I think you bottled it!" says Lord Sugar.

With everyone severely underwhelmed, it comes down to the actual orders. Nothing from the department store for either, but luckily an online retailer placed an order for 250 of the girl's jackets. An unconvincing win, but a win nevertheless.

The treat was to fly water jet-packs at Surrey Docks. In the onsite interview, Katie agreed that everyone was shying away from responsibility and that she would in future be putting her hand up for everything. On the Boys Team, Robert got fired even before the selection of the Final 3. Later, Scott the PM got fired, too.

Week 3: 'Home Fragrance'

17 Candidates Remain

The task is to come up with a Home Fragrance Product, and both teams choose scented candles. They have two days to turn hot wax into cold cash. Katie takes charge as Project Manager of Team Tenacity, and makes it clear there isn't going to be any nonsense. However, her team pushes back when she sets the price above the market norm! Meanwhile Roisin is Project Manager on Team Summit, but despite nailing a substantial order from one of London's luxury brands, falls short on the margin. In the boardroom, Katie's team scrapes a win!

In an unprecedented capitulation, Lindsay confesses that she doesn't feel she can measure up, and Lord Sugar enacts a Mercy Killing, whilst Nurun gets fired from the losing side.

The first couple of Boardroom firings were a big wake-up call for me. It was all very vivid now, and the mood in the camp was beginning to turn from one of *how to excel* to *how to survive!*

Next came Task 3; the Candle Task, which was one of the defining moments of the whole Apprentice process for me. On the day of the briefing I woke up with an absolute determination to be Project Manager, irrespective of the task itself. I didn't care if it was relevant to my experience; I just knew it was my time to make a break for the front of the pack.

I needed to put myself forward for two main reasons. Firstly, I wanted to stand out and show Lord Sugar that I could take it on and succeed. Secondly, I felt like the previous two tasks had been done badly. Even at this early stage, in the girls team there was a clear consensus that people were shying away from being Project Manager because of the automatic exposure to firing if we lost.

If everything went wrong, as the losing Project Manager you would be right in the firing line. So when we got to The Royal Exchange for the briefing, Lord Sugar decided to mix up the teams, which was inevitable. I stayed with the original Team Tenacity, which now consisted of Lauren, Ella-Jade, Sarah, Steven, Daniel, Felipe and Gemma. I recall feeling quite happy about the line-up, even though I felt that Sarah and Steven were a little bit off the map and unpredictable. But all in all, I thought we had a good, solid crew.

In the midst of this briefing, hearing what the task was all about, I realized that the most important thing was to *listen* carefully to what Lord Sugar had to say, because he always gave us a direct message about the primary objective for each assignment. I knew we'd missed the mark on the first two tasks, and I wanted to be sure that I at least had a firm grasp of what he was actually looking for from our performance.

The main message that came through loud and

clear was that this task was all about *profit*; that there was money to be made here, and the word *margin* totally encapsulated what it was all about. After he'd dismissed us from the briefing and we went off for our usual pre-task brainstorm, I thought to myself, "*This is candles; home fragrance. How do I angle this to make sure that the team pick ME for Project Manager?*"

The only way I could think is that I am a consumer of this product. I love candles, and I buy endless plug-ins. That was my angle, and I was pretty sure that most of the others weren't that keen. Straight away, as soon as we all sat down, we had to decide who was going to be Project Manager. I shot my hand up, and pushed my way forward by admitting that I'm obsessive about the smell of my home! I told them that I use the products. Whether it was my forcefulness, or the fact that everyone else was running scared of the PM exposure, nobody else volunteered, and they were happy for me to take it on.

So we were off and running. We had a really focused brainstorm, and I split the team in two. My sub-team set off to deal with the product manufacture, and I sent the other sub-team to get started on the Market Research and Branding exercise.

From the very beginning, I'd made my mind up how this was going to go. I know people always tell you to listen to market research, but the fact is that when you're under the cosh, desperate for a result, it's only human nature to ask such open ended questions that the information you get back is all about consumer aspiration. People always want *everything* until they're put on the spot to spend their own money. Almost invariably, especially with everyday commodity products, most people will select on the basis of price!

I knew that if we were going to have a chance at winning this task, we needed to make something cheaply and then sell it at a high price. So as I was looking through my list of options in the car, en route from the briefing to the factory, and I had to make a choice between two different kinds of wax for the candle-making process. On the one hand there was paraffin wax, and the other was soy wax. The soy wax was environmentally friendly, which could have been a powerful selling point. The paraffin wax might give off a sooty flame, but it was much, much cheaper.

I'm sorry to say it, but I'd already made my mind up. The *margin* word was front and centre in my mind, and frankly it wouldn't have mattered what came back from the market research, I was having paraffin wax!

I started looking at the different options for the glass vessels that we would be putting the product into. Of course I was interested in the aesthetics, how the candles would look, but was there going to be a big difference in terms of customer appeal, whether we used a funky square jar or something simpler? I had Felipe calculate the differing volumes of wax that each vessel held, and I chose the round glass because it held significantly less. So now I had the cheapest ingredients and the smallest displacement volume.

Later in the day, I got the call from the sub-team, reporting (as expected) that the Market Research was telling them people wanted the soya wax and a funky shape. The consumers were being given all the options, and of course without any pressure to buy anything, they were asking for the luxury option every time!

I told the sub-team that I'd made my 'executive decision' and I knew from their reaction that they were far from happy. In their context, they had every right to be upset, but I was determined to lead the team to victory and my plan was fully formed, so I stuck to my guns. Apart from the solid commercial logic that I applied, I also knew that if we failed, and I ended up in the boardroom, at least I would have a clear justification for the decision I had made. One that I instinctively knew Lord Sugar would appreciate.

I had a mantra in my head, something Mam had said to me many times as I was growing up in her business. She told me that *'no decision is a bad decision! It's always a good decision if you can justify why you made it.'*

Despite making a very cheap, yellow coloured candle, called *British Breeze* (even though it didn't have a single British ingredient) we won the task! Anyone who watched the program, and the boardroom dissection of the respective teams' performances, may recall that we won by the narrow margin of £14. But the other team had sold all their stock, and we had a mountain of stock left over; so had it been a real business, we would have been able to go out again the next day and turn that essentially free stock into a huge additional profit. Which would have counted for nothing if we'd lost! Phew.

I love winning. That day was incredible. The feeling was just massive! To win as project manager was huge, but more significant for me was that I had demonstrated to the other people in the process that I was a real contender. I was willing to take risks and make decisions, I had a business head, and even though I didn't spout all the jargon, I could do it. That's the day I put my stake in the ground.

So, with that great win under my belt, we moved onto task four, which was to prove memorable for all the wrong reasons!

Week 4: 'Fat Daddy'

15 Candidates Remain

The task is to make and launch an online video channel. The criterion to win is to have the most views on YouTube in the first 24-hour period. Team Summit, led by Solomon, decide to make a wacky cookery show. Meanwhile, Team Tenacity, led by Ella-Jade, decides to go for fitness. Unfortunately the concept doesn't play well in audience research, which feeds back that they feel it might be classed as insulting or prejudiced towards the overweight population.

In the boardroom, it's announced that Team Summit have the most views, and Team Tenacity are left facing defeat. Not content to let the process play out, outspoken Canadian Social Worker Steven demands to be made Project Manager for the next task, and Lord Sugar promptly and unceremoniously fires him on the spot. Leggy blonde Sarah, she of the short skirts and red lipstick strategy from Task One, also falls out of favour and is fired. Then, in a further unprecedented shock, Lord Sugar completes the triple by firing the losing Project Manager Ella-Jade!

Online Video Channel

The briefing for Task Four was to create a YouTube video. The objective was to make it 'go viral' and the criteria was a simple as it could be. Whichever team got the most views over the stated period would win, and as Lord Sugar loved to say, in the losing team, at least one person would be fired!

As Lord Sugar was briefing us, I was thinking *'this is mine!'* Whereas the previous task had been one of pure strategy, this was right up my street because it was so similar to a lot of the stuff I do in my own businesses. I wanted to be Project Manager again, but unfortunately on this occasion, he chose the leaders without any input from the teams themselves! *Damn!*

When we sat down for the brainstorm, there were some great ideas flying around. Ella-Jade, who was PM for the task, decided to go with *"Fat Daddy Fitness Hell"*. I was dying inside. I knew that we could come up with something much better, but she was in charge and that was her choice, so I had to fall in line. Once it was decided, I thought that maybe it might have some legs, and on the basis of the name it could go viral. But it was clear that to make it work, it needed great execution.

As the task went on, I felt myself becoming more and more withdrawn from the process. The concept was poor, but I really wanted to get behind the team and not moan about how I really felt, so I decided to throw myself into it as much as I could, even though I had huge reservations.

We got through it, in the way that most people get through a root-canal operation. It was horrid.

The next day we were back in the board room, with no idea whether we'd won or lost. I was terrified that if we had lost, and if I was the one to get fired, my career would have been in tatters. After all, I'm the fitness guru, and even though I hadn't led the task, I was the only player in the team who knew the territory. It was clear throughout that people were looking at me for the technical input for what was essentially a very poor fitness video. *It should have been mine!* And if it had been, I would have approached it in an entirely different way.

To get fired that day could have been really detrimental to my business and me in the future. No pressure then!

I wasn't confident that we'd won, and as it turned out, we hadn't. We weren't beaten by much, but neither team covered themselves in glory, at least as far as Lord Sugar was concerned. I was knotted up inside from the moment we arrived at the boardroom door. I was thinking to myself *"There's no way on earth you can get fired on this one. You have to fight your corner. If you get fired today, that's your career in the toilet."*

I knew that Felipe was worried, too. His concern was a little different. He was terrified of getting fired then turning up at his daughter's school gate, knowing that every other parent had seen his ritual humiliation, not only in the character of Fat Daddy, but also getting booted off the show. He'd been swept away with the task, but the reality was setting in. Both of us were on the edge that day.

As luck would have it, both of us survived. Ella-Jade, who had led us to an ignominious defeat, was gone.

Week 5: 'Coach Tours'

12 Contestants Remain

The task is to set up and operate tourist Coach Tours. The teams are now thoroughly mixed, with loyalties divided from the original set up. Katie finds herself teamed with Daniel as her Project Manager, who shoots for high-end tours of Oxford. But Daniel's management style hardly meets with universal approval from his team members.

Meanwhile, Sanjay's Hampton Court tours include the added bonus of a rather tacky singsong on the bus, which does nothing to enhance the customer feedback.

Despite everything, including a full-scale rebellion in the boardroom, Katie once more finds herself on the winning team, and on the losing team, James receives a serious dressing down from Lord Sugar, but Gemma is the unfortunate one who becomes the ninth boardroom casualty.

Week 6: 'Board Game'

11 Contestants Remain

The teams are tasked with producing a new board game, which they must market to the retail trade in London. Katie is now joined with the team led by Pamela, who come up with a rather unimaginative (and dare one say sexist/patronizing) concept called "The Relationship Guru" (typical question: "Women dislike which food the most? Pizza, Carrots, or Chicken Salad?").

Meanwhile the opposing team, led by James, invent "GeoKnow" a geographical family question and answer game, which seems to meet with great approval, although they do get their wires crossed when Bianca promises local exclusivity to a small hobby shop in London's West End, thereby cancelling out any opportunity to sell to some of the biggest retail flagships in Europe.

Despite this faux pas, they emerge victorious, and Katie finds herself on the losing side, but escapes the boardroom. Project Manager Pamela is the tenth casualty.

Week 7: 'Advertising – New York'

10 Contestants Remain

The task is to launch a new soft drink in America, with a TV advert, and an electronic billboard in Times Square. Each of the teams split in two. Half the players head for New York. Bianca, the opposing Project Manager, invents "Big Dog", which hardly meets with universal approval from the home-based production team.

Meanwhile, Katie is once again teamed with Australian Mark as PM, and Daniel, and they go for a health drink called 'Aqua Fusion'. Short on originality, and short on brand impact, they are overwhelmed by Big Dog.

As evidence of her consistent performance, even on the losing side, Katie isn't invited back to the boardroom, and after sparks fly between Mark and Daniel again, Lauren, the Manchester lawyer, becomes the eleventh boardroom casualty.

Week 8: 'Hot Tub Wars'

9 Contestants Remain

Country Show

Finally, contestant James gets his hands on the reins of Team Summit, and almost universally screws it up, with a combination of forgetfulness and duplicity. Meanwhile, thrust together again, Mark, Daniel, and Katie under the leadership of 'Fat Daddy' Felipe, prove a winning, if volatile combination. Despite almost coming to blows throughout the task, the team emerges victorious by a huge degree of magnitude. Back in the boardroom, a bloodbath ensues. James's deceptions are uncovered and he becomes the twelfth boardroom casualty.

The next significant task for me was Number Eight. This was the Royal Bath and West Country Show, which most people will remember as the battle of the hot tubs! Going into the task, I was really happy with our team, and I was praying that Lord Sugar would leave well alone. I wanted to stay with Mark, Daniel, and Felipe, because I knew that we were really strong. We were all on the same page, ticking along nicely, and I didn't want to see things mixed up. Luckily, I got my wish.

I really fought my corner to be Project Manager because I felt that I knew the team inside out, understood the dynamics, and I had a good sense of what each of the members was good at. It was also time for me to raise my profile once again. Of course, it was a testosterone-laden crew. The guys were all about telling the world what they could do, whereas my approach was to take a step back and observe each of them, so I could figure out their real strengths and weaknesses, not just what they thought about themselves.

Unfortunately, they went all tactical when it came to choosing the PM. The boys knew full well that I could manage the team, and if I say so myself we might have avoided some of the nasty confrontations had I been in charge. But I think that Mark and Daniel felt that Felipe was the weak link, and that if they made him PM and we lost, he'd be the easiest person to throw under the bus. Such is the way that everyone evolves on the Apprentice. Whilst there are lots of people in the process, it's easier for the strong guys and girls to protect themselves, simply by outperforming the weaker candidates. But as we were now getting down to the last few tasks, tactics began to play a bigger part, and a few little ruthless streaks were starting to emerge.

But even though I really wanted the job and pushed myself forward, it didn't happen. Never mind. Crack on.

When Daniel and I were at the show, meeting all the vendors, the barbecue guy, the lawnmower guy, and finally the Hot Tub guy, there was absolutely no doubt that the Hot Tubs were the big prize. He had hot leads coming back the next day, he'd already done great sales to that point, and that was the one for us. After we'd pitched him and were waiting for our phone to ring to tell us whether he'd selected our team or the others to work on his pitch the next day, the suspense was killing us.

We were freezing cold. It was the end of the day and we were shattered, but the adrenaline was flowing. When we got the call, he really spun out the decision. He told us how much he'd liked Daniel's passion, and that I was really intelligent, and eventually he told us that we would be selling his tubs the very next day. We were ecstatic!

In my head, it made perfect sense for Daniel and I to go and sell the hot tubs. We had won the deal in the first place, and I was confident that we would do a good job. But, of course, Aussie Mark had a different view of the world, and unleashed his most ruthless and uncompromising side to secure himself a place on the team that clearly had the hottest product. For better or worse, Felipe caved to Mark's pressure, and I really felt for Daniel, because he was unceremoniously done over by what could really only be described as undue influence and management weakness. I wanted to stick up for him, but I didn't want to push the point too much, because this task was very much about individual performance, and in the worst-case scenario

Felipe could decide to dump me, and send the two boys to the Hot Tubs. Plus, I never forgot that the cameras were capturing everything!

This was the point in the process where it all started to get really tactical. Nobody was thinking about the team any more; everyone was focusing primarily on themselves. However, once Mark and I reached the pitch and got started, we just sailed through it. It was the best day I had in the whole process, working with Mark. He was lining up lots of appointments, sending them over to me, and I was converting them. We had people queuing up to talk to us. We nicknamed ourselves *Team Matey*, for Mark and Katie, and we were flying; systematic, efficient, and above all successful.

Of course, even though it felt good to us, we had no idea whether we'd won or lost until we reached the boardroom. Nothing was confirmed because all the sales we thought we'd made were subject to overnight credit checks, so no matter how we'd performed on the day, there was always the possibility that the deals would not complete. We also knew, sitting in the boardroom, that if we lost we were all in danger, because we had fewer people on our team than the others. But if we succeeded, it had the potential to be the win of the series.

In the event, we beat the others by a country mile. It was the biggest win of the season, and the second biggest win in the entire history of the show itself. It was huge. We sold over £30,000 of hot tubs. Just one tub that *I* sold was seven grand.

It was a fantastic feeling to win so convincingly. The task demonstrated to me that the preconceived idea I'd always held about *selling* was a far cry from what was really working for me. I'd always thought that you had to be a slick, car-salesman type of person to succeed in sales, but what I discovered was that the key was firstly knowing the product inside out, which by the end of the day we certainly did, and secondly it was about customer empathy. Once I knew my product and what the customer really wanted, it became a simple case of matching the two together. It was more about nudging them along gently to get them to something that they wanted, and could afford, than it was about steam-rolling them. I could have shown them the complete range of five products, but that would have been a waste of time. My strategy was to listen to the signals, what they were actually telling me, and then to lead them to the solution without going round the houses.

It was a key lesson for me. It opened my eyes to a different kind of business to mine, and it's a huge takeaway from the process that I know will help me in the future. But above all, I'd made it through another week, and contributed visibly to the team's success. The Apprentice is not a points-based system, because that would be boring and predictable, but if it had been, my score was high that day!

Week 9: 'SkeletonGate'

8 Contestants Remain

'10 Years of Discount Buying'

Shocked awake by the presence of Lord Sugar in the house, a motley collection of contestants line up in pajamas to be told that they are going on the traditional Apprentice 'Scavenger Hunt', which this time reprises nine of the most unusual products featured in the previous shows. Katie's team remains intact, with Mark, Daniel as PM, and Felipe. The objective is to buy each of the items at the best possible price, and bring them all back to the boardroom by the deadline...

On to the next task - the Scavenger Hunt. We had to find products all over London and bring them back on time. I felt that our little team had really worked well, and after the previous win we'd even managed to bury the hatchet between the boys, who had really fallen out over the hot tub allocation and subsequent events. But Daniel had changed a lot, and learned to praise other people and see the value in his colleagues. Felipe and Daniel had kissed and made up after their disagreements. Mark and I had been a good combination every time we'd worked together.

We walked the task. We were the first team in Apprentice history to get back to the boardroom on time with all the items, or so we thought. I'd never been so sure of a win in my life as I was that evening.

Picture this. We're sitting in the boardroom, with Lord Sugar in the middle as Karen and Nick read out the numbers. Who was late? Who was on time? We had won by a country mile. We were already at the backslapping stage when out of the blue, Lord Sugar held up his hand. *"Hang on, hang on..."*

For those that missed it, one of the items on the list was an *anatomical skeleton*. In hindsight, it's clear what was required; one of those full-size artificial skeletons that are always at the corner of the hospital lab on TV. Daniel and Felipe had taken on the half of the list that featured the skeleton, but instead of bringing back a fully built up model, they'd managed to source a flat-pack version, made of dozens of cardboard pieces.

Now, it's arguable that had they taken the time to construct the thing, we might have got away with it. But, unfortunately, the task was against the clock and so that was impossible. Lord Sugar was apoplectic and as much as Felipe fought his corner, the boss's word was final. He not only disallowed our IKEA skeleton, but also fined us as if we'd failed that part of the task, and gave Felipe a dressing down to boot. People tell me it was TV Gold, but I have to tell you that sitting there and watching it unfold, as a clear and unequivocal victory was cruelly snatched away from us, my chin was on the floor.

That one item cost us the task. I couldn't believe it. But at that moment, I realized that I had only one chance to get through to the following week, because at least one of us was going down the road that evening. I didn't care how I was going to do it, but I was determined that I wasn't going to fail because someone else had bent the rules.

But I was devastated. On the way to the loser's café I cried my eyes out, which was the first and only time I'd cried in public since the start of the process (all the other times, I'd had my head under the blankets, missing home). I wasn't sad or scared; I was supremely frustrated at what had happened. We didn't deserve to be there. We were by far the stronger team, but we'd been undone by a freakish anomaly, which could so easily have been avoided. All I could think was that we'd made Apprentice history; *it shouldn't be like this!*

The production process means that while the losing team is doing their post-match soul-searching in the Bridge Café before going back to the boardroom for the firing ceremony, each member is taken outside for a one-on-one interview. I was so upset that I could hardly speak, and I only managed to answer one question. I just opened my mouth and burst out crying every time!

In the event, Felipe got fired. Looking back, thinking about what I felt about SkeletonGate, at the time it was dubious because it had put me in a weak position, which was not where I ideally wanted to be, heading into Week Ten of the twelve-week process.

In the moment, I was angry like hell, but now looking back with better hindsight, I feel differently about it. I feel like Felipe potentially did do the right thing. He was trying to show Lord Sugar that he could operate outside the box and be a creative, lateral thinker, which was against the accusations that he'd faced in a few of the previous boardroom assassinations. Felipe took a risk that had backfired, but I say good on him for having the nerve to try and outsmart the smartest guy in the room, Lord Alan Sugar!

It's entirely possible that we would have gotten away with it under different circumstances, but given that our 'modified interpretation' of the rules may have won us the task, there would have been hell to pay from the other team if the result had been allowed to stand, and that would have compromised the apparent fairness of the entire process.

Wound-licking time!

Week 10: 'Premium Pudding'

7 Contestants Remain

Throughout the Apprentice process, over the previous ten weeks, I had been speculating, particularly with Roisin, that the next assignment would be a catering task of some kind. By the time we arrived at week ten, with just seven of us left, I'd pretty much written off the possibility. Because I was pitching a restaurant business to Lord Sugar, I felt that it was important that I got to demonstrate that I had, at least, some comprehension of the food and drink business!

So when we arrived at the briefing, and Lord Sugar explained the nature of the task; that we were to be making and marketing premium desserts, I knew that this was 'the one' and I had to push myself to the forefront as Project Manager. Luckily, it all came together because of my business plan. The boss chose me as the PM, and Roisin as the PM of the opposing team.

We started our briefing. Sanjay had swapped into our team, and Daniel had moved across to Summit, so there was a new dynamic, and it was no longer testosterone-driven by the rivalry that the boys had been unable to sideline thus far.

We made some great decisions at the start, and we got good momentum from the get-go. I decided that *my* focus should be on the product creation and the manufacturing process, and I sent the boys in the sub-team off to do the branding.

Over the task, everything fell into place. Anyone who watched the show will recall that this was the task where ace-salesman Mark, who was to be the eventual winner, had his famous coughing fit in the middle of the Tesco pitch, which was messy, but it was the only negative issue that we faced, despite it being a key feature of the televised version of events.

We arrived at the boardroom. I realised that if we were to be the losing team, I would be in trouble, not only for the standard reasons of having been the defeated PM, but also because I had been selected to do the job because I was claiming to have some expertise in the catering business. Despite the fact that I wasn't really interested in the dessert sector, I knew that nobody would give me that leeway, least of all Lord Sugar. This was a food-related task, my opportunity to shine, and it was as black and white as it could be.

There was also an anomaly in as much as we only had three members in our team versus four on the opposition; so if we lost, the chances of getting fired were amplified even higher. And if that was not enough, the next stage of the competition was to be fought out by the final five contestants, so it was almost certain that there would be two firings that day. Clearly, there was a huge amount riding on winning this task.

We lost.

The moment the announcement was made, I knew my fate was sealed. I had been in charge of a food task, and I'd failed. The writing was on the wall. It was obvious to me that no matter how hard I might be willing to fight for my survival, the game was probably up.

For the first time in Apprentice history, the issue of contestants' Business Plans was the central point of discussion in the boardroom. As this had never happened before (Business Plans were not previously revealed until the brutal Interview Round, which was the following week), there was a lot of commentary after the event, particularly in interviews, about whether I thought it was fair. Actually, under the circumstances, I did. It may be counter-intuitive, but in that particular task, because we had lost with a solid performance, Lord Sugar would have found it impossible to point the finger at any one of us as being the reason why we had failed, so the fact that there was a clear-cut focus on me, both as PM and as the one with the Catering Business Plan, there really wouldn't have been a fairer way of deciding.

So I sort of knew what was coming. My dread was not at being fired; after all I'd come an enormous distance to get ten weeks into the process. I was more worried about how we (I) might be savaged for actual performance, and that would have meant ending on a very sour note.

In fact, that wasn't the way it played out on the

day. Lord Sugar was thoroughly pleasant in the way he handled it. He told me that I'd shown him a lot of common sense, and that I'd been a very strong candidate. It was 'with regret' that I was being fired; a gentle let down. He wished me well in my ongoing business career, as did Karen Brady.

When I left the boardroom and walked out into the foyer, I started crying uncontrollably. Of course I was absolutely gutted, because I'd come so close that I could almost touch the final. But actually it was more about pure relief on reaching the end of what had been the most pressure I'd ever experienced. Nothing I had ever done in my life had measured up to the relentless day-in day-out demands of the Apprentice process, and although I'd grown and adapted to handle it (and even got off on it to some extent), when it was lifted so abruptly, my tears were all about the release!

I cannot envision ever being in such a pressurised situation again. That's not to say I wouldn't welcome it, because I learned throughout that process just how resilient I am, and about capabilities and strengths that I may never have otherwise discovered. But I certainly won't be going looking for that kind of pressure in the future.

Afterwards, all I wanted to do was go home. I didn't want to stay one more night. No more hotel rooms or strange beds. I felt like I was in limbo, because I was obliged to stay, but I was desperate to get back to Sunderland and reconnect with my real life, right away.

One thing really stood out for me after the firing, and that was how wonderful the production team had been. There were lots of hugs and commiserations. Even though I'd got on quite well with the other candidates, the bonds were stronger with the various people on the crew. They truly understood what we were going through, and consistently bent over backwards to make sure there was no additional pressure coming from the mechanics of the production, over and above the process itself. Without exception they were all consummate professionals, and I really enjoyed the time we spent together in the crazy, surreal Apprentice world.

When I got home, Mam, Dad and Simon put on a little party for me, which was lovely. But even then, and for about a week afterwards, I felt totally detached. Sure, I was physically in the room with people that had known me all my life, but mentally I just wasn't finding it easy to make the transition back to real life.

Every waking moment was spent re-running the experience; every element and scenario; getting myself all chewed up inside; trying to find the moments in time where I might have done something different which could have changed the end result. In my head, I replayed the final boardroom over and over again, wondering if I could have done it better. My logical self always knew that it was water under the bridge, but my emotional self was battling with what had happened, maybe trying to come to terms with what was technically a failure, after such a long run of successes.

Mam asked me several times if I was all right, and commented that she felt like I wasn't really there. She said, "You've come home, but you've left *you* back there in London." She was right.

It took me quite a while to get back to normal, if there really is a normal any more. After the sustained stress and different reality, I was affected on levels that I couldn't even identify. If I had to use one word to describe how I felt in those first few days and weeks, I was *lost*.

I'd gone though this unique experience that only people who've been there could ever fully comprehend. I couldn't talk about it to anyone whilst it was happening, because of strict confidentiality clauses, so nobody close to me understood what I was feeling. Even though I'd spent seven weeks, during which I'd never actually been on my own, I was emotionally isolated from all my anchors.

Even after my Apprentice firing, apart from my closest family, I still couldn't talk to anyone about it, because the whole process was still secret.

Before I'd left for the Apprentice, I hadn't been allowed to tell anyone where I was going, and after I got back I had to continue to perpetuate a grand deception that I'd been in Marbella to train a celebrity, which was my cover story. I even had to get a spray tan so that no one would question if I'd been there or not.

Surreality piled upon surreality!

Although the TV show runs chronologically over twelve sequential weeks, that's not the whole story, which is why the secrecy is even more important and strictly enforced.

I came home at the end of June. The show didn't start airing until the end of October. It was a little later than it had been in previous years because the BBC wanted to avoid any scheduling clashes with the soccer World Cup, which was the flagship of summer 2014.

It truly was 'over before it began'. Such is the magic of the TV time warp!

Three days after I got home, the production team asked me to come back to join one of the support teams for the final itself, which was filmed. As an aside, I thoroughly enjoyed that part of the process, because the pressure was off me personally. However, even that final task was in the can by mid-July, and would not actually be aired until mid-December.

Even the finalists, having duked it out, and having been left in the boardroom for the benefit of the TV cameras, would not find out which one of them had actually won until December 18th!

So if you think it was bad for me, sitting at home, chewing over everything that had gone on, just try to imagine how Mark and Bianca had to deal with waiting six months to find out if they'd won or lost.

That's the magic of television.

Once I was over the disappointment of not winning, I wanted to make the most of the experience. I knew that it had the potential to boost my business if I could figure out how to leverage all the elements. It was a once in a lifetime opportunity, and it was vitally important to jump right onto it whilst there was something there that I could use for my own professional benefit. Here, the time lag worked in my favour, because it gave me several months to start putting things into place to take advantage once the show actually aired.

I threw myself into it. Every day I was working on my e-mail marketing strategy, my follow-up material, my pitches; I started sharpening up my social media, my website, new online products ready for my new followers, and a keynote presentation that I could use to launch myself into public speaking. I knew the effect wouldn't be everlasting, and my shelf life would be limited. But the timeline was set in stone, and it was up to me to take maximum advantage of the exposure that I could gain from being a part of such a massive hit TV show. It was a huge opportunity.

Talking to other candidates, both from this season and previous shows, a number of them seem to have made the error of believing that the TV exposure in and of itself would bring opportunities flooding their way. Whilst there undoubtedly are opportunities out there, if you don't go and find them you're not maximizing your potential.

I also wrote a format for a fitness TV show that I then pitched to my regional independent TV channel, and they bought it, which was fantastic. I might never have had the working knowledge of the TV industry to have the confidence to make that pitch, had I not spent half the year surrounded and immersed in the Apprentice experience.

If there's one huge lesson that I took from my Apprentice experience, it is that things don't always turn out the way you envision but, in any process, there is always an outcome, and if you can recognize the by-product opportunities, there's a lot you can do to turn disappointment (or even relative failure) into future success.

I didn't win the show, but I still emerged a winner.

9: And... Breathe

So I was back. And once I'd worked through my decompression phase, things started to come together.

The first thing that I put in place was my public speaking strategy. I'd often done speeches and presentations within the fitness industry, such as workshop days, either self-hosted, or as a guest at someone else's event. I was a confident speaker on health and fitness. Sometimes, I was speaking to the public, but more often, I had been talking to fitness professionals about the latest training techniques, running a fitness business, and anything to do with attracting and servicing clients.

I was very comfortable in that zone; confident, and outgoing. But now I felt that I had another story to tell, and a different audience that I could tap into: fellow entrepreneurs and people starting their own businesses. I had some good examples of things that had been successful, and that I knew would help other people in a similar situation. But where to begin?

A good friend of mine, Geoff Ramm, who's a well-known public speaker, had been on to me even before the Apprentice, suggesting that I should speak to Michael Arnott at the Unique Speaker Bureau. But before the show, I hadn't felt that I had a particularly compelling pitch. However, once I came back, I was more confident. Geoff had repeatedly told me that there weren't many good, young female speakers on the circuit.

I got in touch with Michael and set up a meeting. It was the day that I was finally able to go public about my participation in the Apprentice. To cut a long story short, since that day I have been inundated with speaking gigs, in colleges and universities, business networking events, all kinds of different events. Of all the goals that I set myself this has been the one that has surprised me the most. Before I went into the TV show, I was hustling to get on the platform to speak. Since coming back, things couldn't be more different!

I have had the pleasure of working with some big brands, too, such as Very, and Reebok, fronting their *New Year New You* campaign. PomWonderful, the rapidly growing Pomegranate Juice vendor, also picked me up for an online campaign.

One of the big things I'd always wanted to achieve was to get on TV with my Health and Fitness message. My fitness businesses have been very successful in giving me a good living, but the whole fitness space is my overwhelming passion, and to be able to broadcast on a bigger platform was always my aim. It's not a job; it's my life. By being on TV, I knew I could reach a much bigger audience and improve their lives. I also knew I would never be able to recruit everyone to a class or a gym, but if I could only reach them, I could encourage and motivate them to make some kind of change that would be better than the way they were before.

Only TV can do this.

For a long time, I had been thinking about an idea for a TV show of my own. I'd watched all the fitness shows throughout my life, such as Biggest Loser and Gladiators, but I always felt they were very sensational. I wanted to do something that was more down to earth and accessible for people. There had to be a challenge, and I needed to find people who would be willing to go through the challenge. People with whom the viewers could actually identify.

In the event, I found a wonderful group of people; Alison, a new Mum; Gemma, who'd been through a really stressful time in her life and gained a lot of extra weight; Jeremy, who'd recently bought a chocolate shop and also had too many after-dinners on the speaking circuit - a thoroughly diverse group of people. I wanted my viewers to look at the class and think, "those people are just like me."

I didn't just want people to watch it, but to get involved, too. The second half of the show would be me delivering an actual home-workout to the viewer that they could join in with. I discovered that there was a new regional channel starting in my area, called 'Made in Tyne & Wear'. I thought to myself, *'What's the worst that could happen?'*

All I needed to do was to find a way to get in front of someone and pitch my idea. Whoever the guy is, I wanted to show him what I was planning, If he didn't like it, fair enough, I'd find another way or a different angle, but I knew if I didn't give it a shot, I would always be wondering what if... So I checked out the website, found a telephone number, and called.

I got a ten-minute meeting with the Station Manager, and what do you know, he loved it!

To cut a long story short, the first series is now running, and they've already asked for a second series. What's more, the feedback has been amazing. It seems that what I wanted the show to be turned out to be exactly what people wanted to watch; real people struggling with real weight and fitness issues, and to see results for themselves in their own lives, which has definitely been the outcome so far.

So that was big tick in the box. Alongside the product endorsements and filming for the big fitness brands I now work with, and the launch of the TV show have been amazing career opportunities. I'm not saying that they would never have happened without Apprentice, because I'm a determined girl and I don't give up easily. But there's no doubt that the doors opened a whole lot easier with the Apprentice on my CV.

How on earth did Reebok ever trust little Katie from Sunderland to write and execute a fitness program for them, a huge global brand? It's a wonderful feeling; nerve racking for sure, but truly amazing.

For the future, now I have my platform firmly

established, I am determined to use the public profile I've been fortunate enough to acquire to drive me forwards to achieve even more. The doors I had been pushing on before are now wide open. Speaking, TV, Brand Marketing, all of these are paying well and are (extremely) enjoyable. The Apprentice gave me the huge push I had been looking for to reach the next level.

My Dad asked me the other day what I'm planning to do next, and it's hard to answer. One thing I know is that if it all went away tomorrow, I'd still be extraordinarily happy, because I've achieved so many things that I was only able to dream about in the early days. And I'm not thirty yet.

Having set up my pathways, now I'm intrigued to follow them and see where they lead. I have a 'Vision Board' with my goals, and I've crossed so many of them off.

There's a lot of emotion, too. All the things I worked so hard to achieve have finally happened.

I made a few good friends in the Apprentice process. Roisin is a real friend and we speak often. I'll always keep in touch with Bianca; these two were real professional career women. As for the others, I'll undoubtedly keep in touch with them all and I'd always sit down and have a drink with them if we met, but so many of them were from different walks of life, and working their way up such diverse career paths, that I guess it's inevitable that we'll steadily lose touch over the years ahead.

And Finally

I've learnt an awful lot during my time in business and as an Apprentice candidate, but there are several lessons that particularly stand out, which I will never forget and will always live my life by...

1. It's cool to be yourself! You do not have to conform!
2. The more successful you become, the thicker your skin must grow.
3. Do what YOU love, no matter what anyone says.
4. Believe in yourself and there is nothing you can't achieve.
5. Other people's opinions and worrying about what your competitors may say does not pay your bills... so just do it!
6. Family first.
7. It's nice to be nice!
8. Keep your feet on the ground.
9. The way things are is not the way they have to be
10. See the people and not the pound signs and you'll never be poor!
11. Shy bairns get nowt (if you don't live in Sunderland, that means if you don't ask, you don't get)
12. Nobody is better than you, and you are not better than anyone else... we all use the toilet!

13. And finally, inappropriate clapping can change your life!

Connect with Katie

www.katiebulmer.com

www.thefitmummymanual.com

Facebook: Katie Bulmer-Cooke

Twitter: @KatieBulmer1

Instagram: katiebulmercooke

E-Mail: katie@katiebulmer.com

Download my free health and fitness app.

Simply search Katie Bulmer Cooke in the App Store or Google Play.

More about Katie

Fitness entrepreneur Katie began her journey in the world of business at the age of 16, setting up exercise classes in her home town of Sunderland. Fast forward 11 years and Katie is now selling her fitness DVDs and online training programmes in the US, Australia, South Africa, Japan, New Zealand and Mexico as well as educating her fellow fitness professionals on how they can grow their businesses.

- UK Personal Trainer of the Year 2012

- UK Fitness Professional of the Year 2013

- Top 10 Global Personal To Watch 2012

- Sunderland Young Business Person of the Year 2012

- *The Apprentice 2014* Candidate (made it to week 10 of 12)

- Health & Fitness Expert for Argos

- Brand Ambassador for Reebok

- Programme Creator & Consultant for Reebok, Very.co.uk (fronted their New Year New You campaign), *POM Wonderful*, PT500

- Sold my business model *The Little Black Dress Club* to 39 UK locations and 1 in Canada all without leaving my back bedroom!

- Kate Middleton gave royal recognition to my post-pregnancy fitness DVD

- Fitness DVDs sold internationally (Australia, New Zealand, Japan, France, South Africa, UK, Canada, US)
- Master Trainer for GymCube.com
- Presenter of *Total Tone Up* (now in third series) on Made TV (started as a regional show on Made in Tyne and Wear and due to viewing figures has now been aired across their national network)
- Published in *Top Santé* Magazine's *100 Hottest Health Gurus* alongside Tracy Anderson and Matt Roberts (Madonna and David Cameron's personal trainers)
- Also published in *FHM, Workout Magazine, FitPro, Bella, Women's Weekly, The Sun, Holland & Barrett Magazine,*
- Regular guest on *Capital FM, Sun FM* (voiceover artist), *Metro, Smooth, BBC Newcastle, The Week*

Last Word from the Ghost

When Katie and I first talked about this book, she was in the middle of the Apprentice TV series, or so I thought. As you have learned, in the world of TV Reality Shows, nothing is ever quite what it seems! There was a great deal that Katie couldn't tell me; nevertheless we embarked on telling her story together. She knew where it was headed; I had absolutely no idea!

It turned out to be a pleasure to write with Katie. Her natural enthusiasm for everything and everybody is truly infectious, and it's clear to anyone who meets her that she's successful because she gets things done.

Thanks Katie, I had a ball!

Rick Smith, London, June 2015.
rick@ricksmithbooks.com

44405547R00074

Made in the USA
Charleston, SC
26 July 2015